Of all the monastic rules, perhaps the most valuable is the Rule of St. Benedict

"Marked by common sense in every instance, the *Rule* makes success in a man's quest for God seem not only possible but eminently probable.

"The sanity of Benedict's approach gives added force to his central vision of the quest. He sees it as an ever-expanding, enriching exercise of love. Communal life provides each member with the support and comfort of a family in which monks are brothers, sons with Christ of God, and of the abbot whose name means father.

"For the man of the twentieth century, rootless and isolated, such a vision may need transformation before it can be made real, but its appeal is undeniable. Here is his Father's house, the center of light and warmth. Here are his brethren, united to each other by love and their quest for the God he seeks, and thus united to him. He may not be able literally to seek their sanctuary and shelter within its walls, but the spirit that guards them, strengthens them and makes them one is his for the asking and receiving."

—from the *Introduction*

D1011819

The Rule of St. Benedict

TRANSLATED,
WITH INTRODUCTION
AND NOTES BY

Anthony C. Meisel
and
M. L. del Mastro

IMAGE BOOKS
DOUBLEDAY

NEW YORK LONDON TORONTO SYDNEY AUCKLAND

AN IMAGE BOOK
PUBLISHED BY DOUBLEDAY
a division of Bantam Doubleday Dell Publishing Group, Inc.
666 Fifth Avenue, New York, New York 10103

IMAGE and DOUBLEDAY are trademarks of Doubleday,
a division of Bantam Doubleday Dell Publishing Group, Inc.

Library of Congress Cataloging-in-Publication Data
Benedictus, Saint, Abbot of Monte Cassino.
   The rule of St. Benedict.
   Translation of Regula.
   Bibliography: p.
   I. Meisel, Anthony C., 1943–
II. Del Mastro, M. L.   III. Title
BX3004.E6   1975   255'.1'06   74-33611
ISBN 0-385-00948-8

Contents

Acknowledgments

We wish to thank Dean Alden Sayres of the New School of Liberal Arts, Brooklyn College, for bringing us together and encouraging our work; our colleagues, especially Bruce Park and Douglass Roby, for their constructive criticism; Norman F. Cantor for his usual concern and advice; John Delaney and Theresa D'Orsogna of Doubleday; and Susan Meisel and Adela Garcia-Bird.

Introduction

Monasticism is the quest for union with God through prayer, penance and separation from the world, pursued by men sharing a communal life. The energy generated by this kind of living produces effects within the individual member, within the community and to some extent upon the world at large.

Flourishing for a thousand years, Christian monasticism had spectacular effects in all three areas. Mystics, saints and miracle workers were frequently numbered among the inhabitants of monasteries. These members seemed to grow holy together, drawing upon one another's virtues to combat their own weaknesses. And the monastery itself frequently became the center for spiritual inspiration and guidance throughout its area as the sanctity of its members became known.

More visible than these (and in some ways more accessible to the twentieth-century observer) were the effects of Christian monasticism on the world around it. These effects were rich and varied: theology, philosophy, art, architecture, music, science, history—all were marked and some were reshaped by the contributions of the monks. Christian monasteries assisted in the growth and protection of the Church, nurtured and preserved art and learning when these were threatened with destruction, and fostered developments in agronomy and the practical arts. In the process monasticism became a politically potent, intellectually vibrant and artistically rich force which transformed Western civilization.

The power that effected that transformation was the monastic ideal. It marked the man who embraced it with a fierce single-mindedness. Seeking only the glory of God and union with Him, the monk saw everything he attempted as a step nearer his goal. Consequently, he brought all his talents and every resource of his person to bear upon its accomplishment.

Since his primary goal was union with God, the material results of his work were less important to the monk than the growth in virtue that accompanied them. Undistracted by desire for visible success and fear of failure, the monk was able to concentrate all his energies upon the task at hand. He was freed from the enticements and terrors of the world and its values and from the tyranny of his own passions by his desire for God. Refusing to be the slave of the material universe, he became its master. As a result, he moved in serenity. A leisure of spirit marked all he did with the sign of freedom and peace.

For the man of the twentieth century, such serenity and freedom would be treasure indeed. Harried by the things of his world, he is pressured by conflicting demands on his time, strength and patience. He is frightened by the anarchy that boils beneath the social, political and economic surfaces he strives to keep whole and in place. He feels himself to be victim, not master, of the forces of a hostile universe. Unable to control these energies, to shape them to his will, to use them to replant and cultivate the garden for which he longs, he is buffeted by them. He is swept from the security of a firm place in an ordered universe to the chill dark of an isolated, meaningless existence. He has somehow been cut off from his sources and is not sure how or even if he can return to them.

For such a man what has monasticism to offer? The certainties of the monk are not his heritage. Can the monk's serenity and freedom be then available to him by the monk's means? Is the monk's quest for God, so direct in approach, single-minded in execution, available to him under any circumstances? Perhaps.

The mode in which he pursues it, of course, will be, as it always has been, determined by his past experiences, his talents and temperament, and the circumstances under which he finds his life must be lived. Nevertheless, he will be amply repaid by an examination of the monastic patterning of the quest, not so much for its details and the adjustments necessitated by communal living (though these have their own value in other contexts) as for its spirit.

Of all the monastic rules, perhaps the most valuable in this context is the *Rule* of St. Benedict. Marked by common sense in every instance, the *Rule* makes success in a man's quest for God seem not only possible but eminently probable. The calmness of tone and moderation in counsel accord well with modern man's sense of how life ought to be lived. At the same time they promise him respite from the harassments he actually must endure.

The sanity of Benedict's approach gives added force to his central vision of the quest. He sees it as an ever-expanding, enriching exercise of love. Communal life provides each member with the support and comfort of a family in which monks are brothers, sons with Christ of God, and of the abbot whose name means father.

For the man of the twentieth century, rootless and isolated, such a vision may need transformation before it can be made real, but its appeal is undeniable. Here is his Father's house, the center of light and warmth. Here are his brethren, united to each other by love and their quest for the God he seeks and thus united to him. He may not be able literally to seek their sanctuary and shelter within its walls, but the spirit that guards them, strengthens them and makes them one is his for the asking and the receiving. For finally that spirit is Spirit—God Himself.

ORIGINS IN THE EAST Though centered in and grounded upon the Divine, the *Rule* itself is a product of men. To understand its impact on the Middle Ages as well as its significance for the twentieth century, we must go back to its beginnings.

Retreat from the world in a life of penitential asceticism to foster union with God or express fidelity to Him was not a Christian invention. The Essenes, who lived such a life in the wastelands of Judea, flourished at the time of Christ as a well-established phenomenon. John the Baptist, who "lived in the wilderness" and "wore a garment of camel-skin and . . . lived on locusts and wild honey," (Mk. 1:4–7) seems to have been one of them.

Christians of the first and second centuries, however, seem not to have taken this direction in their following of the Master. Small communities, suffering, after the first few years, bitter and prolonged persecution, provided for them ample scope for practice of the two commandments Jesus had named as greatest: "You must love the Lord your God with all your heart, with all your soul, with all your mind and with all your strength," and "You must love your neighbor as yourself." They were separated from the world already, and quite effectively, by its often bloody hostility. They had no need to seek the wilderness in flight from its blandishments! Those who wished to imitate the Lord by virginity and other ascetic practices seem to have done so within the community, and indeed, within their own homes.

It was not until late in the fourth century that monasticism, properly so called, was established as a separate entity set apart not only from the world but from the Christian community as a whole. Of the complex of causes that provided impetus for this development, three deserve special mention.

In the political sphere the Roman Emperor Constantine I, a Christian catechumen baptized before his death in 337, gave Christianity official recognition and imperial patronage in 311 with the *Edicts of Toleration*. The imperial patronage and frequent favors he bestowed on the religion and its adherents from then until his death gave to both a security and status never before granted to followers of Christ. The Church and many of its members found Christianity and the world quite compatible.

Those who did not felt impelled to withdraw from immediate interaction with both, though they continued to regard themselves, and to be regarded, as Church members. The Egyptian desert proved a welcome refuge for these ascetics, and they tended to live there as hermits in caves, excavated tombs, temple ruins and the like. In so doing, they were carrying on a mode of life that had been practiced there since the close of the third century.

For the second thrust in the development of monasticism, we look to philosophy, and in particular to Origen of Alexandria, a Church Father who died in the mid-third century (254). It was Origen's desire to express the Christian experience as an orderly, rational pattern of perfection based upon sound philosophical principles. Origen saw man as co-operating in the process of his own sanctification, the outcome of union with God. He further saw the process of attaining holiness/union as an ascent to be accomplished by steps or degrees. These steps had to be taken by a man. His only access to these stages of development was the unremitting practice of asceticism. The image of the ladder irresistibly suggested itself in connection with this concept, and the combined concept and image quickly became an indispensable element of ascetic thinking and living.

The optimistic Origenist conviction that a man could help himself to attain his heart's desire—God, salvation, sanctification—had for a corollary his responsibility to do so. The combination of "I can/I must" proved superbly effective as an energizer in the ascetic life. It drew men to make the attempt, and supported them in continuing it through difficulties.

The third force that lent vigorous assistance to the growth and development of monastic ideals and practices was the decline and disintegration of the Roman Empire at the end of the fourth century. Waves of barbarians poured over the frontiers, flooding the provinces remote and near. Their growing power threatened Rome, and civilization itself seemed on the verge of extinction. Those who had welcomed the alliance between Christianity and the powers of the world were given pause. Suddenly the illusion of stability and solid security that political and economic prosperity had created shimmered and started to dissolve. Transience and impermanence were once again operative realities. Christians were forcibly reminded that their Kingdom was not of this world.

For a man caught in such a situation, there seemed only two alternatives. He could continue to pursue material goals single-mindedly, ignoring the warnings of futility the barbarian successes reiterated. Or he could turn his energies to the quest for God and eternal rewards, letting earthly gain fall to its appointed dust. Many Christians in the East chose the latter course. A number of these fled to the Egyptian desert.

Their enthusiasm was supported and encouraged by the example of several famous ascetics who lived there as hermits. Of these Antony the Great, who died at 105 in 396, had perhaps the greatest influence.

We learn of Antony through Athanasius, Bishop of Alexandria, who wrote his life. Athanasius too was preoccupied with the pattern of Christian perfection. He presents in the *Life* the picture of the ideal ascetic, progressing step-by-step (shades of Origen!) to sanctification and union with God. Asceticism and self-denial were the means by which Antony reached the spiritual heights. His movement from level to level of virtue was reflected in his movement by stages from the society of men to the solitude of the hills east of the Nile. His warfare was against the devil in all his Satanic activities. His victory, won first and effectively by Christ and thus assured, was the work of his lifetime. Thus, the principles of Origen had flesh-and-blood expression in Antony's desert. Men found them compelling.

They also found them ample cause for fear. The desert and the solitary life therein were not easy to endure. Robbers, real and hallucinatory demons, temptations, boredom, anxiety, despair, physical privations and excessive penitential watchings, fasts and prayers combined to destroy the unwary and the proud with frightening ease. Fear of destruction, which had driven many to the desert in the first place, threatened to drive them away from this haven which had promised so fair a salvation. But there was no place left to go.

Pachomius, a countryman and contemporary of Antony and for a time a Roman soldier, is credited by a fourth-century tradition with finding a solution for the dilemma—the cenobitic or enclosed communal life.

According to his *Life*, which reaches us through Jerome's translation, Pachomius created a communal kind of eremitical life. He built a wall around the huts of his ascetics, separating them from the world and joining them to one another. They came together for spiritual instruction and worship weekly. They were united by their observance of a *Rule of Life*. Thus, they were free to pursue their individual quests for perfection and union with God without the anxieties and dangers found in desert solitude. Pachomius did not legislate minimal ascetic practice or place limits on an individual's penitential zeal, preferring to let the Spirit guide each as He willed. Prayer and contemplation were treated in similar fashion. Manual labor was performed by all for the benefit of all. The discipline and order created by Pachomius' *Rule* served to free the ascetics, not to stifle them. It simply established a rhythm for living within which each man could become progressively more fully himself because more fully his God's.

The practical values of communal asceticism were evident to the ascetics of the fourth and fifth centuries. In the area of Judea there sprang up the *laura,* an association of hermits living in cells surrounding the cell of an especially holy or well-known ascetic. The *laura* was communal in the extended sense. The individual hermits looked to their leader for advice and spiritual direction, but not for group legislation. Frequently these associations developed into cenobitic communities and flourished.

It remained for Basil of Caesarea (d. 379) to provide for the cenobitic life a solid theological grounding. In both the *Longer* and the *Shorter Rules* Basil's paramount concern was with the building and fostering of community life. He did not despise the hermit's way of solitude; indeed according to his friend Gregory of Nazianzen (Sermon xliii, 62), he established both individual hermitages and *laurae.* But he was careful to place these retreats for solitary contemplation in fairly close proximity to houses of cenobites, so that men pursuing these separate paths in their quest for God might be kept in touch with each other to their mutual support and profit.

Basil saw the religious community, the cenobitical life, as the only place in which the true ideal of Christian perfection could be completely realized. Only the community could meet the insistent needs of soul and body. Only the community provided its members with the opportunity of ceaselessly exercising fraternal charity and humble self-sacrifice—the instruments by which the soul is freed from the tyranny of its own selfishness and its body's passions. Only the community with its diverse gifts of body and spirit could accept and be transformed by the gifts of the Holy Spirit in their fullness. Within the community the individual was to exercise his talents and let his gifts illumine his brothers, while he shared in the effects of theirs.

Basil saw the divine economy of salvation working at its most effective level within the monastic community. His *Rules* can be seen as an amalgam of all that was best in the development of the monastic ideal in the East.

SPREAD TO THE WEST The cenobitical and eremitical ideals of Eastern monasticism found their way to the West by a variety of routes, some of which were so unexpected as to verge on the bizarre. If illustration were needed that "God works in mysterious ways His wonders to perform" the history of Western monasticism would provide a full range.

To begin with there was the influence of Bishop Athanasius and his biography of Antony the Hermit, which we have already examined as an influence on Eastern asceticism. This work also made an enormous impact on the Western mind, though had events followed their normal course nothing of the kind would likely have occurred.

Athanasius, the Bishop of Alexandria, was exiled from his diocese by Arian Christians. These heretics denied the divinity of Jesus and the virginity of His mother, but accepted Christian ethical teachings. The bishop, a staunch supporter of Roman orthodoxy, made his way north to Treves (335) and Rome (340). He made friends there before returning south to go into hiding in the Thebiad.

There between 356 and 360 he wrote the *Life of Antony*. The book became popular at once, and by 370 it had been translated into Latin by Evagrius. This made it accessible to the West where its popularity continued. Augustine of Hippo described his discovery of it through his countryman Ponticianus, and his amazement at its contents (*Confessions*, VII, vi).

Augustine's response to Antony's life was not unique. The appeal of desert asceticism and the cenobitic life had caught hold in Italy and several monasteries were already flourishing. Ponticianus told Augustine in particular of one in Milan. Jerome (*Letters* CXXVII, 5) writing in 412 reports on one in Rome that followed the *Rule* of St. Pachomius.

From Rome and Italy the ideal of desert asceticism and the practice of the cenobitical life spread to the farthest reaches of the crumbling Roman Empire. The transmitters were chiefly three: Martin of Tours, Augustine of Hippo and John Cassian.

Of these, the first is largely a figure of legend. Martin, the Roman soldier who gave half his cloak to a beggar only to see Christ wearing it that same night, is in large measure the creation of his biographer, Sulpicius Severus. Severus had in full measure the hagiographer's habit of appropriating to his subject any wonder, virtue, motive or miracle that happened to be lying about, as long as it made good "copy." We cannot rely very heavily upon him for literal truth and factual accuracy.

Of the "real" Martin, consequently, we have little knowledge. That he had an impact on his times and that a large part of that impact was monastic in the Egyptian ascetical mode, we can judge from the historic results. An Egyptian form of monasticism flourished in Tours, which combined the eremitic with the cenobitic life. And the fame of Martin's life and miracles, spread first by Severus

(d. c. 420), then by Gregory of Tours (d. 594) and finally by Venantius Fortunatus (d. 600) is solidly connected by all three with the introduction and development of this monastic tradition. Further, Western monks looked to Martin as an exemplar, and many monasteries were named after and dedicated to him.

Since he wrote no rule for his followers, we have no way of knowing how much of the monastic practice at Martin's Tours was shaped to the norms of desert asceticism and how much was adapted to meet the needs of the harsher northern climate and quite different Germanic temperament. The experience of other monastic leaders, recorded in their rules and other writings, indicates that in all probability Martin too had to compromise. Martin's increasing fame in the years that followed his death, taken together with the flourishing of the Tours foundation, indicates that whatever compromises were made were successful.

The second and third of the transformers of Eastern monastic asceticism to the Western mode left records in addition to foundations. Augustine of Hippo and John Cassian each took the heritage of Eastern desert monasticism and grafted onto it elements that would enable it to survive transplantation to the West and would allow it to flourish there for a thousand years.

Augustine saw the combined reality of obedience and authority functioning to form the perfect common life. This for him was essential to success in the soul's quest for God and sanctity. Though he had been exposed to and impressed by the ideal of the solitary ascetic in Antony, Augustine seems to have preferred the cenobitic life he saw led in the monasteries of Milan and Rome for his own living. Baptized at Milan in 387, by 388 he had sold his patrimony and joined with a few friends in leading a monastic common life.

Although he continued this style of living with his clergy after he became Bishop of Hippo (394), Augustine wrote no rule for these brethren that has come down to us. What we have of his ideas on monastic living is found chiefly in three places—the treatises *Concerning the Work of Monks* (*De opere monachorum*) and *Concerning Holy Virginity* (*De sancta virginitate*) and a letter (CCXI) of 423 written to one of the communities of nuns he had established. The last-named was quickly adapted for use by communities of men. "Filled in" judiciously from the other two works, it became the *Rule of St. Augustine* which proved so useful to so many different groups in the later Middle Ages. It was in *Letter CCXI* that the principles of communality, obedience and authority, which were to become staples of Western monasticism, were enunciated.

For Augustine the community life with its demands upon the faith, charity and mutual service of its members was the surest way to achieve perfection. The community was to absorb all the energies—physical, psychic and spiritual—of all its members whose individual perfection lay in the perfecting of the life of the whole. Augustine's nuns, it appears, were destroying one another and their common life with the corrosives of bitter internal strife and jealousy and the fires of vindictive party warfare attendant upon (and causing) rebellion against an appointed superior.

The bishop's first response was to reprove and correct this dangerous misconduct by pointing out its perils and consequences. His second, with which we are here concerned, was to reaffirm the principles of the supremacy of community life in the attainment of perfection and of the authority and responsibilities of the superior together with the concomitant duties of the subjects.

In regard to the first, Augustine reminded his chastened audience that they were supposed to be seeking the perfection of charity. Their progress in this virtue could be measured by the degree to which they habitually chose the common good, the good of the whole community in preference to personal good (§12). Such choice entered all the traditional areas of cenobitical life, serving as a kind of "first principle" in the quest for perfection. Thus, common life became the only means by which the quest could be successfully pursued. This, at any rate, is the impression left by the letter. It is this impression that has shaped much of Western monastic living, even to the present time.

Since Augustine's first principle of the common good placed such emphasis upon the common life as the primary means of sanctification, it followed that in his scheme of things the role of the superior as binding force of the community would require special development. With a vigor that probably derived as much from the practical needs and demonstrated weaknesses of this particular community of women as from philosophical necessity, Augustine insisted upon the supremacy of the superior and the breadth of her authority. These derived, according to the bishop, from her weighty responsibilities. She was to be held accountable by God for the practice of virtue in the community and for failures therein. Since the individual members could approach perfection only if the community as a whole did, she was also to be held accountable for the sanctification of each member of the house and would have to answer to God for each soul that had come to it.

This double responsibility of the superior for the life of the community and the salvation of its members removed one kind of responsibility from the members and placed another upon them. Since the superior was responsible for their salvation, they, in turn, had the duty of obeying her "like a Mother" lest, as Augustine warned them, they offend God in offending her (§15).

A significant change in the ascetical pattern occurred here, thanks to Augustine's anxiety to insure the stability of community life. To the superior's traditional duties as guide and assistant to the questing ascetic climbing the Origenist ladder of perfection, were added the burdens and responsibilities of parenthood. The ascetic was reduced from an individual, independent or semi-independent, seeker after God to a child, owing obedience to a parent and finding his salvation only in total submission both to that parent and to the community of his brethren. The consequent loss of independence was compensated by an increase in security expressed in the formulation that while the superior could err in commanding, the subject could not in obeying. This notion had enormous effect in shaping monastic life, and persisted without significant change or challenge until Vatican II.

The third of the transmitters of the traditions of desert asceticism to the West is John Cassian. Cassian at heart was a follower of Antony. Trained for a short time in monastic living in the community at Bethlehem, he and a companion had sought (rashly, Cassian later admitted) and obtained permission of the elders of that community to make a pilgrimage to the desert. They wished to observe the ascetic life and penitential practices of the hermits and cenobites, in order to bring these back to Bethlehem.

Once in the desert, Cassian was overwhelmed by the spirit and practice of desert asceticism, decided that he could not transfer these successfully to Bethlehem and resolved to remain in the desert to live this life. The resolution was not to be fulfilled. In 399 Cassian unwillingly left the desert, under what circumstances we do not know. He was never to return.

From what we can learn of the details, a dispute between Origenist Greek-trained philosopher-monks who insisted upon the transcendence of a God who was Pure Spirit, and Egyptian Coptic monks who tended to anthropomorphic simplicity in their worship, with bitter recriminations and persecutions on both sides, seems to have been involved in Cassian's removal to Constantinople. Ordained there against his will as deacon (c. 403), he, with other Origenist and foreign monks from Egypt, attached himself to the bishop of the city, John Chrysostom.

The latter's forthright and uncompromising championship of the expelled religious, and his promotion of them to positions of authority in the diocese over native sons, seem to have contributed to his own downfall, without significantly aiding their cause. By 405, with Chrysostom deposed, Cassian had headed for Rome, and by 415 he had been ordained priest and was living at Marseilles. There he founded St. Victor, a pair of monasteries (one for men and one for women), in which the members led as nearly as possible the ascetical life of the Egyptian desert.

About 420 a near neighbor of Cassian's double foundation, Bishop Castor of Apt, asked Cassian for help in founding a similar monastery. It was in reply to this request that, between 425 and 430 Cassian wrote his *Institutes* and *Conferences*, both for Bishop Castor's monks and for his own at St. Victor.

In these two works Cassian provided a pattern of monastic living that combined the best of what he had observed of the traditions of Egypt, Mesopotamia and Judea (*Institutes*, Preface, pars. 5–9). Gaul was not Egypt, however, nor were its inhabitants Eastern in temperament or training, and Cassian knew it. Hence, though he believed the eremitical ideals of the Egyptian desert to be the perfect monastic way of life, and their ascetical practice the program best suited to bring about the union of man with God, he tempered their severity.

In addition to providing a coherent program, which placed the best of Eastern asceticism in a Western context, Cassian developed the notion that the *coenobium*, the communal monastic life, was a permanent rather than a temporary state for the average monk. Traditionally considered a school for beginners in the spiritual life, the monastic community had been used in Egypt as a pre-eremitical training ground. Men would begin their spiritual formation within the walls of the community, and when they and their superiors felt they had achieved adequate spiritual maturity, they would head for the desert and the semi-independence of the eremitical community. Within that loose association of ascetics, each would pursue his own program of sanctification.

Cassian subscribed to the theory underlying this practice. He saw the *coenobium* as a mediocre way of life meant for beginners and achieving its perfection in the loftier state of the hermit. At the same time, however, he discouraged his monks, by word and example, from entering upon the perils of the solitary way. The solitude of the desert was for the perfect man not the sinner—and who would presume to declare himself perfect?

The monk should be grateful, Cassian had Abba John remark in *Conference XIX*, for the advantages of the communal life. It guarded him from the dangers of vanity by immersing him in the company of his brethren. It ensured the eradication of his self-will—the cause of his sinfulness—by subjecting him in all things to the will of his superior.

Thus, Cassian, in effect, established the living of the communal life as an end in itself and a means by itself for the attainment of perfection, though he maintained the superiority of eremitism. He seems to have arrived, for other reasons and by other routes, at some of Augustine's conclusions.

LIFE OF BENEDICT   The most effective synthesis of Eastern and Western asceticism, however, was made by Benedict of Nursia (480–547).

Of Benedict himself we know only what Gregory the Great (c. 540–604) tells us in the second of his *Dialogues*. Present scholarship indicates that this biography is as much legend as Severus' *Life of Martin*, perhaps for the same reason. In both cases, the hagiographer was moved by didactic rather than historic considerations. For Gregory, the moral implications of an event and its effectiveness as a teaching device were the criteria for its inclusion in the *Dialogue*, itself a means of educating. Since he was clearly more interested in the inculcation of virtue than the dissemination of verifiable fact, the author must be approached with considerable caution as a historical source.

According to Gregory's account, Benedict was the son of a distinguished Italian family. Born in Nursia (c. 480), Benedict was sent as a young man by his parents to complete a liberal education in Rome. There he was struck by the ease with which his fellow-students were being destroyed by vice. Frightened, Gregory tells us, lest he should likewise be destroyed if he continued in the pursuit of worldly wisdom, Benedict abandoned his studies, gave up his home and his inheritance and entered upon the single-minded quest for God.

The route he chose was that of penitential solitude. First at the Church of St. Peter Affili with his faithful nurse, then alone for three years in a cave at Subiaco, the young man grew in virtue and closeness to God. Gregory gives no indication of the particular program the young

Benedict followed, noting simply that it involved separation from the world, abstinence and much prayer.

His needs were met by the charity of several persons. Romanus, a monk from a near-by monastery under the Abbot Deodatus, had met Benedict on his way to the cave at Subiaco. He had agreed to keep the hiding place secret and tried to supply Benedict with food and clothing as well as he could from that which was supplied him for his own needs by his monastery.

Gregory also tells the story of a priest whom God summoned to share his Easter dinner with Benedict and the tale of the shepherds who, seeing him in his cave wrapped in animal skins, at first thought him a beast, but later fed him as a servant of God.

It was with these last that Benedict began his work of healing souls, but not before he had been purified of the vice of lust. Assaulted by a peculiarly violent temptation, Benedict, responding to the grace of God, Gregory reports, rolled naked in a nettle patch. The pain of the stinging nettles was sufficient to drive out the temptation completely, and never again did he experience another temptation of this kind.

Freed from temptation, Benedict was able to instruct others in the practice of virtue. At the start this instruction seems to have been chiefly verbal. People came from the surrounding areas asking for advice or assistance in spiritual and temporal matters, and Benedict supplied it.

Then came the first group of monks to ask him to serve as their abbot. Though he warned them that their way of life and his would never harmonize, they insisted, and got a good deal more than they had bargained for! Benedict as abbot insisted upon strict monastic discipline of body and spirit and exact observance of the monastery's rule. He would tolerate none of the former waywardness and disobedience. They grumbled and sulked.

At last, weary of Benedict's unceasing efforts to reform their lives, curb their vices and faults, and change their settled and apparently lax habits of mind, the sullen monks tried to poison their abbot. They failed due to a miracle. As Benedict blessed the pitcher containing the poisoned wine, Gregory reports, it shattered "as though struck by a stone." Observing this Benedict realized what had been plotted against him. Having said the equivalent of "I told you so!" to the thunderstruck brethren, he returned with delight to his solitude.

He was not to enjoy it for long. As the fame of his sanctity spread and, says Gregory, because of his signs and wonders, disciples began to gather around him. Much as ascetics had gathered around the fathers in the Egyptian desert, they sought his counsel and guidance in their search for God. He banded them into communities and soon he had founded twelve monasteries "with an abbot and twelve monks in each of them" (§3). He seems to have headed his own community at the same time for, says Gregory, "There were a few other monks whom he kept with him, since he felt that they still needed his personal guidance" (§3).

For the rest of his life Benedict was busy directing the monks in these monasteries. Gregory focuses his narrative on the "signs and wonders" the saint performed, particularly in the realm of second sight and prophecy, though more physical miracles were also recorded. The point of the miraculous incidents seems to be that the saint abhorred sin of every kind and could always detect it in the sinner.

The sins so detected were chiefly those of disobedience, especially as these involved appropriation by the individual of goods properly belonging to the community. These same areas were stressed in Benedict's *Rule*, though Gregory makes no mention of the connection.

In all cases the saint's response was the same. He would confront the offender with the details of his hidden or forgotten offense. The monk invariably would admit his guilt and repent of it at once. Then Benedict would forgive him. With a warning against future transgressions and provision for restitution where this was indicated, he would restore the offender to the charity of the common life.

Benedict died of a fever in 547. He was buried next to his sister, the nun Scholastica, in the Chapel of St. John the Baptist in Monte Cassino. Gregory recounts the "signs and wonders" associated with the death and burial of Benedict with his usual enthusiasm. These included a prophetic foreknowledge by the saint of the day of his death, a vision of his path to heaven granted to several brothers and cures of every description.

THE *Rule* OF ST. BENEDICT It is just before his account of Benedict's death that Gregory mentions the *Rule* the saint composed. In Gregory's view, the *Rule* with its "discretion and clarity of language" (§36) was the demonstration of Benedict's wisdom in teaching. His judgment has been amply substantiated in the 1,400 years since the *Rule* was first implemented.

Perhaps the greatest strengths of the *Rule* are its common sense and its evident love and concern for the welfare of the individuals who would embrace it as a way of life. In composing his *Rule* Benedict drew upon Eastern and Western traditions of asceticism and reshaped them into a new creation.

Benedict saw the monastery as a primary school in religious asceticism—as had Cassian—but also saw it as a perfectly desirable end in itself, not a second-best, if necessary, alternative. He addressed himself not to the hermit or the cleric, but to the layman who knew that no matter how hard he tried he would be a "beginner" for the whole of his life's pilgrimage.

Benedict saw the common life as the most perfect instrument of salvation and sanctification for such men. The mutual support of brothers striving for the same end —union with God—was most necessary for beginners in the pursuit of perfection. The demands on charity and humility communal life provided in abundance were salutary both for the respondents in the virtues they strengthened and for the recipients in the gifts they conferred.

The common life as Benedict envisioned it enabled each individual to achieve the fulfillment of all his potential. It allowed each man to draw upon the strengths of his brothers to supply for his weaknesses. It was to no one's advantage to have monks leaving the cloister for the hermitage, though this was admittedly a higher way of life for those who were called to it, and the use of the monastery as a way-station was actively discouraged.

Again like Cassian, Benedict adapted monastic practice and regulated the daily pattern of work and prayer pragmatically, but did so without regret or condescension. He legislated few specific variations in custom, preferring to rely upon the common sense of the abbot for proper adjustments.

Consequently, Benedict was most particular about the qualities the abbot ought to have. With Augustine he saw the abbot as father (hence the name), and the monks as sons to him and brothers to each other. He agreed with Augustine that responsibility for the practice of virtue in the house devolved upon the abbot. Likewise, he saw the abbot held eternally accountable for the virtue and salvation of each of his monks.

To fulfill such a responsibility, the abbot had to be wise and prudent, but more important he had to excel in the practice of virtue himself. Otherwise, how could he direct others to the pursuit of virtue and prepare them to avoid the pitfalls set for the unwary?

Though he had authority over the others, the abbot had no right to pride but ought the more assiduously seek after humility. But he was not to sacrifice the necessary exercise of his powers of command lest anarchy result and the community be destroyed.

Most important, the abbot had the obligation to love his sons the monks and to exercise this love by encouraging and assisting them in their quest for God and perfection. This might require that the abbot reprimand and punish as well as praise and comfort. He might have to enforce unpopular and difficult decisions for the good of all as well as mitigate too harsh customs. In any case, he was not to seek the praise of this world but the approbation of heaven and to remember that pleasing both simultaneously was a flat impossibility.

Since the monks were to be sons in Christ to the abbot, they owed him obedience in all things, in Benedict's as in Augustine's opinion. The difference seems to be that while Augustine saw obedience as one virtue among many, with love as the most important, Benedict saw obedience as the single reality, the master virtue. It was the perfect expression of man's human nature, with all other virtues operating as aspects of it.

As brothers to one another, the monks were, of course, to practice charity in forbearance, patience and mutual respect, but all was to be done at the direction of the abbot or with his consent. Thus, the dangers of ill-regulated or pseudo love were to be avoided.

The chief work of the monks as Benedict saw it was the *opus Dei*, the work of God. This formal, communal worship service, which is described more fully in the Notes, was to punctuate the monastic day and night with periods of prayer. Praise to God and instruction for the brethren were combined rhythmically within each prayer period or "hour" (*hora*). Each had its own particular character. In addition, each day's prayer entered into the liturgical worship of the Church universal, reflecting the cyclic alternations of penance and joy. It was in the *opus Dei* that community life found its primary expression, and in periods of silent prayer that this expression found its life.

The rhythm established by the *opus Dei* was counterpointed by communal work. As in the *laurae* and among the desert eremitical communities, every monk had his tasks to perform. He contributed to the survival and smooth functioning of the community. For the monk of St. Benedict, the needs of the monastery and his own talents determined the nature of the tasks he would perform. He was subject to the rhythms of the earth and the patterns of darkness and light in his work as he was to the rhythms of the Church in his formal prayer. Together the patterns formed a whole and healing life rhythm. The dynamic balance of forces allowed each man to become his best self if he chose to submit to them.

A third element in the Benedictine life was intellectual activity. Monks were encouraged to read and study in order to learn from Scripture and from those who had preceded them in ascetical living. Not for Benedict the Egyptian fear of books! Whatever would help a man to grow in virtue and self-knowledge, broaden his understanding of the mysteries of God, enrich his prayer and deepen his union with Christ was to be used without fear. Especially recommended were the lives of the desert fathers, and Cassian's *Institutes* and *Conferences*. Though his monks were not desert ascetics, they could learn much of value from these holy men and ought to do so.

A fourth contribution made to the development of Western monasticism by the *Rule* of Benedict was the vow of stability. This promise had a double effect. By it a monk promised to remain until death in the community that had accepted his profession. Thus, stability ensured the permanence of the monastic foundation itself as well as the relative fixity of its population. By this vow Benedict eliminated the vagabond tendencies that had marked Egyptian eremitical ascetics. He also warred against the tendency to make the monastery a first step in the process of a man's becoming a hermit, rather than the permanent resting place for the man who saw himself as beginner in need of community support in his life-long quest.

More important, by the vow of stability Benedict had brought mobility—the physical expression of a man's pride, independence and self-will—under the healing influence of obedience. The course of perfection, as Benedict saw it, could only be completed successfully if self-will were annihilated and replaced by the Divine will. To this end, stability proved a remarkably effective means.

Finally, with stability came peace and security, essential conditions for the consistent practice of virtue by the individual and the community.

The *Rule* Benedict composed took from East and West the best elements, harmonized them and built from them a perfectly balanced communal life of prayer and work. This life was intended to serve as a living miniature of the Church of Christ. It was an image of the Christian life as it ought to be lived, made of men, living flesh and spirit. The image was also reality, with eternal implications.

IMPACT OF THE *Rule* The *Rule* Benedict composed for his monks had a great influence on the development of Western civilization. Its common sense, compassionate awareness of the limits of human endurance and coherence as an ascetical program recommended it to its contemporaries. The *Rule* was frequently adopted in combination with other rules, notably those of Columban, Basil and Cassian, as it traveled from Italy through continental Europe. In almost every such case, the *Rule* became the only rule to be observed. It seemed to compensate for the deficiencies of its partners in such a way as to render these unnecessary.

Benedict died in 547. In 597 his biographer, Gregory the Great, now pope, sent a group of monks from Rome to England. They were to preach the faith to the Angle and Saxon pagan tribes who now controlled this former outpost of the Roman Empire. A long-held tradition (currently under serious challenge) ascribes the bringing of Benedict's *Rule* to England to these monks and their leader Augustine of Canterbury.

The tradition seems to be linked to another (equally old, equally challenged); that Gregory himself had followed the *Rule* of Benedict, both as monk and as abbot in his monastery of St. Andrew on the Caelian Hill in Rome and had sent Augustine and his companions from that establishment to England. While interesting, and much tidier than anything that can be proved, the tradition's truth or falsity cannot yet be firmly established.

We do know that both Gregory and Augustine were monks, and that the monastic life that was familiar to them was brought by the missioner-monks to England. Bede reports in the *Ecclesiastical History* (I, 27) that Gregory urged Augustine and his companions to continue in the monastic practices in which they had been trained. Augustine should live a communal life with his clergy, serving them as abbot. Together they should observe the monastic virtues and "attend to the singing of the Psalter" —the *opus Dei*, in short.

Augustine and his monks did what Gregory had commanded. Wherever they went throughout the length and breadth of England, they brought monastic living.

Whether this was the monastic living prescribed by the *Rule* of Benedict is not at present ascertainable. Nor, finally, is it important. What is known and is important is that Benedict's *Rule* came to England, met there a flourishing Celtic monasticism and gradually replaced it. The *Rule*, observed in combination with one or more Celtic *Rules*, worked its usual alchemy and became the exclusive *Rule*.

The spread of Benedictine monasticism was phenomenally fruitful. By the eighth century England, converted and enthusiastic, was sending her own missioners abroad. They preached the Christian faith to the Germanic pagan tribes that had completed their take-over of Northern Europe. Several of the best-known and most successful of these brought with them in their living the *Rule* of Benedict.

One of these monk-missioners was Boniface; another his predecessor and for a time partner, Willibrord. Between them these indefatigable missioners with their companions brought Christianity and monasticism to a large piece of the growing Frankish Empire under Charlemagne's ancestors.

In addition to missionary work, monks who followed the *Rule* of Benedict were engaged in intellectual pursuits, and particularly in education. Two of the most famous of these scholar-educators were Bede and Alcuin.

Bede (673–735) was an English monk who spent almost his entire life in monastic surroundings. As a child he was entrusted by his father to the care of the Abbot Benedict Biscop of St. Peter's monastery at Wearmouth to be educated. He seems to have been transferred to its sister monastery of St. Paul at Jarrow at the latter's foundation by Abbot Ceolfrid in 682. There he remained as a monk until his death.

Bede's work in the monastic community was education. He taught younger monks and boys, dealing with Scripture and its interpretation. He translated some Scriptural and ascetical works from Latin into the vernacular. He also wrote commentaries on Scripture and on some of the works of the Fathers of the Church.

Perhaps his most notable contribution was his compilation of the monumental *Historia ecclesiastica gentis Anglorum—Ecclesiastical History of the English Nation.* Rather than contenting himself with making a simple chronicle, Bede did his best to gather and collate in this book the written and oral history of Christianity in England. He traced it from its first arrival with the Romans through its second flowering under Augustine to its contemporary eighth-century heights. The work was labor indeed, for Bede insisted upon living or documentary verification for everything he included. Where this was either lacking or contradictory, he presented the information concerned as doubtful. In addition, Bede labeled interpretations of events as such, avoiding the pitfalls of partisan distortion and propaganda. The result of this first attempt at writing what we have come to call history, was remarkable. Tempered, balanced, rational, the *Historia ecclesiastica* made its mark and still serves as a model for objective historical writing.

The second scholar-educator reared in the Benedictine tradition, Alcuin (735–804), had an impact equally great but different in kind on his own and future times. Trained at Wilfrid's monastery at York, which is credited with introducing the *Rule* of Benedict to the north of England, Alcuin absorbed the prevalent love of learning, common life and liturgy with little difficulty. His reputation spread, and in 782 he was summoned by Charlemagne to head the group of scholars that ruler had gathered at his capital in Aachen. From Italy, Ireland, England and Spain the scholars had come to form a court school.

The school was primarily intended for the sons of Charlemagne and of his nobles, but soon came to include talented children from the lower classes as well. The curriculum of this school, and the quality of the teaching were both Alcuin's responsibility.

In addition, Charlemagne used the monk's liturgical training by having him assist in preparing a revision of the *Gregorian Sacramentary*. This *Sacramentary* was intended to ensure uniform liturgical usage and to establish the Roman rite as a replacement for the old Gallic rites throughout the Empire. Alcuin also helped in the preparation of a revision of the Vulgate Bible. He composed exegetical and theological treatises and seems to have invented, or at any rate rediscovered for the Middle Ages, the catechism, which presented the basics of Christian doctrine in question-and-answer form.

The monk's assistance and advice to the Emperor in his programs of educational and liturgical unification of the spreading Empire gave him quasi-political power, and real worldly status. His influence was considerable. His aims tended to coincide with those of the Emperor, who had linked the prosperity of Church and State so firmly as to render them virtually identical.

The result of this union for the monasteries was twofold. First, there was a flowering of the arts brought about through monastic agency. Once the missionary work was completed during the ninth century, monasteries and their monks turned to other activities. They developed a rich liturgy to which music and art contributed as much as they profited. Scholarship flourished with the study of and commentary upon Scripture and the Church fathers as well as other areas of learning. Literature was developed and preserved both in Latin and in the varied vernaculars of the countrysides surrounding the monasteries.

With the increase of monastic holdings of land and

other forms of wealth that accompanied the union of Church and State interests came a growth in architecture. Architects, stonemasons, glaziers, wood workers, metal workers—all these and more found outlet for their talents. They found scope and necessity for innovation and development of their crafts in the construction of monasteries and cathedrals on these new holdings. They built together, they built beautifully and they built well—as any tour, even the briefest, of their still-existing, still-used creations will attest.

The days of glory of the tenth, eleventh and twelfth centuries were also the start of the days of decline. With wealth and status came power, and with worldly power the power of the Spirit is forever at war. Once the monks had cast their lot with the powers of the world and accepted its values, they abandoned the Spirit and His power.

One of the first signs of this shift of allegiance was the treatment of the *Rule*. Upon one pretext or another, prescription after prescription was altered or reinterpreted to allow the monks to follow the pleasures of the world while keeping the name of monks. The letter remained but the spirit was driven out. Like a shell emptied of life, the monastic structure remained, but the works of God had been replaced by the works of men, and corruption of all kinds soon followed.

This was not the end of the *Rule*, however. Benedict had caught hold of elemental truths in constructing his ascetical program for common life. Everywhere men who were in earnest quest for union with God turned to it for guidance and inspiration even as they rejected current versions which distorted it and turned it to worldly ends. Instead of creating new programs, many of these seekers turned to reform, and reform in every case consisted in a return to the primitive simplicity of the *Rule*.

And the *Rule* revivified. Every time a group of men returned to Benedict's ideals and the letter and spirit of his rule, their quest for God and holiness in communal life was rewarded. Perhaps the most dramatic of such returns was accomplished by Alberic and his community at Citeaux.

In this foundation, begun in 1098, Alberic and his monks re-established the monastic essential of separation from the world. They built their enclosure in an isolated spot near Dijon and broke all ties—social, political and economic—that had characterized and corrupted contemporary monastic practice. Returning to the *Rule* for guidance, they simplified the public performance of the *opus Dei*, removed extra public devotions and restored silent prayer and contemplation.

This simplification freed the soul for union with God. It was reflected in the simplification of the Church itself and of the monastery that surrounded it. No towers, no paintings, no luxuries—the soul was to be left undistracted, humble and poor, to pursue the quest for God.

The reformers also reintroduced manual labor and strict poverty. The monks were to do all their own work within the monastery, eliminating the need for lay servants. They were to cultivate their own lands, with the monastery owning only as much as was needed to sustain its members. This eliminated the then common practice of a monastery's owning large tracts of farm land that were worked by servants and tenants while the monks supervised the labor and lived on the profits. Private ownership was, of course, forbidden.

Finally, the houses that wished to follow these observances were to be united by a bond of love rather than one of hierarchical control of founding abbey over foundations. All houses were to be considered as belonging to a single community, observing equally the same customs and equally subject to the same *Rule*.

The impact of the *Rule*, then, may be measured in two ways—in its effects upon the civilization of the West and in its effects upon the quest of the soul for union with God. In both areas, Benedict's *Rule* has been extremely influential as we have seen. The double influence has persisted through the centuries. Scholars, liturgists, musicians, artists, writers, architects, thinkers have peopled Benedictine houses and enriched their times with their talents. And simultaneously, men faithful to the ideals of Benedict's *Rule* have grown quietly holy and sanctified their brethren and their world by doing so. To understand either contribution, it is necessary to examine the *Rule* that gave rise to both in the context of the monastic experience.

TEXT AND TRANSLATION According to legend, the original text of the *Rule*, Benedict's fair copy, was destroyed in a disastrous fire in the monastery of Teano in 896. What has come down to us over the years, with few exceptions, has become confused and corrupted by countless careless copyists and by the peculiarities of the modern reading of early medieval Latin. Even the more reliable manuscript texts exist in a rather disorganized state.

The most acceptable surviving relative of the original is the manuscript *Codex 914* in the monastic library of St. Gall in Switzerland. It was made from a copy of the original. The copy was commissioned by the Emperor Charlemagne for the express purpose of encouraging monastic reform in the Holy Roman Empire. Charlemagne's copy was made, according to the monk Paul Warnefried who wrote a letter to accompany the copy to Aachen (the Imperial capital), from Benedict's original then at the monastery of Monte Cassino. As far as we know, *Codex 914* was copied from the Aachen copy by two monks of the monastery of Reichenau—Grimault and Tatto. When Grimault became abbot of St. Gall in 841 he apparently took the copy with him, and there it has remained to the present day.

Other manuscripts of value, though of lesser authority, are *Hatton 48* in Oxford, *Codex Vindobonensis 2232* in Vienna and the *Codicies Monacensis 28118* and *19408* in Munich.

We have used several editions of the text of the *Rule* in preparing this translation: Philibert Schmitz's edition of *Codex 914* (Maredsous, 1946); the standard nineteenth century texts of the Teubner edition and the *Patrologia Latina* (66); and the most recent edition, A. de Vogüé's (*Sources Chrétiennes*, Paris, 1964–73). The standard text in English has been Cuthbert Butler's critico-practical edition last revised in 1935. Unfortunately, this is long out of print and is slightly dated in light of recent scholarship.

The language of the *Rule* is by no means classical Latin. Benedict was a learned man but he was as subject to the trends of his own time as we are to ours. His language was the Latin of the late Empire; a tongue grown imprecise, careless and ever so slightly corrupt. Those editors who render or correct the language into a more classical mode do Benedict a disservice.

This does not mean his style is without art; Benedict is always clear, logical and forceful and, within the limits of his intentions, sometimes eloquent.

We have been as exact as possible in translation, but we have sought to write clear, contemporary English. However, the text, in literalness and in intent, has always been our final authority. We do not substitute modern equivalents for concepts or objects of Benedict's time without explanation. We have sought especially to convey the spirit of the original. Obviously, we cannot capture more than a fleeting sense of life in the sixth century; but if the reader can be caught up in the period in any way through this version, our efforts will not have been in vain.

Editors' Note

SCRIPTURAL REFERENCES

Benedict, assuming a complete familiarity with the whole of Scripture on the part of his monks, does not identify the biblical texts he uses in constructing his *Rule*. We have preferred to include the appropriate citation in parentheses at the close of each reference, using *The Jerusalem Bible* (New York, 1966) for this purpose.

From Psalm 10 to Psalm 148, the Hebrew Bible numbering of the Psalms (used in preparation of both the King James version and of *The Jerusalem Bible*), is one ahead of the numbering used in the Septuagint and Vulgate versions. Benedict follows the latter system, which joins Psalms 9 and 10, and Psalms 114 and 115, while splitting Psalm 116 and Psalm 147.

In citing Psalm references throughout the text of the *Rule*, we have used *The Jerusalem Bible*. We have not tampered with Benedict's ordering of psalms for the Night Office (Chapter 13) and Day Office (Chapter 18). Citations from *The Jerusalem Bible* have been placed in square brackets following the Vulgate numbers Benedict used.

Listen, my son, and with your heart hear the principles of your Master. Readily accept and faithfully follow the advice of a loving Father, so that through the labor of obedience you may return to Him from whom you have withdrawn because of the laziness of disobedience. My words are meant for you, whoever you are, who laying aside your own will, take up the all-powerful and righteous arms of obedience to fight under the true King, the Lord Jesus Christ.

First, with fervent prayer, beg of Him to finish the good work begun, so that He who has so generously considered us among His true children, may never be saddened by our evil deeds. We must serve Him always with our God-given talents so that He may not disinherit His children like an angered father, nor enraged by our sins, give us up to eternal punishment like a dreaded Lord whose worthless servants refuse to follow Him to glory.

Therefore, let us arise without delay, the Scriptures stirring us: "It is now the hour for us to awake from sleep" (Rom. 13:11). Let us open our eyes to the Divine light and attentively hear the Divine voice, calling and exhorting us daily: "Today if you shall hear his voice, harden not your hearts" (Ps. 95:7–8); and again, "He who has ears, let him hear/what the Spirit says to the Churches" (Rev. 2:7). And what does He say? "Come, you children, and listen to Me: I will teach you the fear of the Lord" (Ps. 34:11). "Run where you have the light, lest the shadows of death come upon you" (Jn. 12:35).

The Lord looks for His workman among the masses of men. He calls to him: "Who is the man that will have life, and desires to see good days?" (Ps. 34:12). And if, hearing this, you answer, "I am he," God says to you, "If you desire true and everlasting life keep your tongue from evil and make sure your lips speak without guile; renounce evil and do good; seek peace and pursue it" (Ps. 34:13–14). "If you do this, My eyes will see you, and My ears will hear your prayers" (Ps. 34:17). "And before you can call out to Me, I will say to you: 'Behold, I am here'" (Is. 58:9). What can be more pleasing, dear brothers, than the voice of the Lord's invitation? See how He shows us the way of life in His benevolence.

Let us encompass ourselves with faith and the practice of good works, and guided by the Gospel, tread the path He has cleared for us. Thus may we deserve to see Him, who has called us into His Kingdom.

If we wish to be sheltered in this Kingdom, it can be reached only through our good conduct. But let us ask our Lord (with the prophet): "Lord, who shall live in Your Kingdom? or who shall rest on Your holy mountain?" (Ps. 15:1). Once we have asked this, listen to the Lord's response as He shows us the way to His Kingdom: "He who walks without blemish and works justice, he who speaks truth in his heart, who has not been deceitful in his speech, he who has not harmed his neighbor, nor censured him, shall dwell with me" (Ps. 15:2–3). He who casts out from the innermost thoughts of his heart the Devil's suggestions for straying from God's path, making them null and void, he who takes his nascent thoughts and dashes them against Christ, as against a rock, shall dwell with Me, as shall they who, fearing the Lord, do not pride themselves on their good conduct. Rather they praise the work of the Lord (knowing that what is good in them is God-given) thus: "Not to us, O Lord, not to us, but to Your Name give glory" (Ps. 115:1). The Apostle Paul attributed nothing of his preaching to himself. "By the grace of God I am what I am" (1 Cor. 15:10). "He who glories, let him glory in the Lord" (2 Cor. 10:17). For the same reason the Lord says in the Gospel: "He who hears these my words and performs them shall be likened to a wise man who built his house upon a rock; the floods came, the winds blew and struck against the house, and it did not fall, for it was built upon a rock" (Matt. 7:24–25).

After the Lord has ended His exhortation, He waits every day for us to respond to His sacred counsels.

So that we may change from our evil ways our lives are lengthened, as in an amnesty. For the Apostle says: "Do you not know that the patience of God will lead you to repentance?" (Rom. 2:4). And "I do not will the death of the sinner, but rather that he be converted and live" (Ezek. 33:11).

We have questioned the Lord, brothers, and have heard of the conditions for living in His Kingdom; but we shall live there only if we fulfill these conditions. Therefore we must prepare ourselves, in body and soul, to fight under the commandments of holy obedience. And that which is less possible to us in nature, let us ask of God—to command the aid of His grace to help us. If, escaping the tortures of Hell, we wish to find eternal life, we must live what God wills in our lifetime, while we have the ability and chance.

We are about to open a school for God's service, in which we hope nothing harsh or oppressive will be directed. For preserving charity or correcting faults, it may be necessary at times, by reason of justice, to be slightly more severe. Do not fear this and retreat, for the path to salvation is long and the entrance is narrow.

As our lives and faith progress, the heart expands and with the sweetness of love we move down the paths of God's commandments. Never departing from His guidance, remaining in the monastery until death, we patiently share in Christ's passion, so we may eventually enter into the Kingdom of God.

CHAPTER 1:

The different kinds of monks and their customs

There are four kinds of monks. First are the Cenobites, those who live in a monastery waging their war under a rule and an abbot.

Second are the Anchorites (hermits) who are not neophytes. They have spent much time in the monastery testing themselves and learning to fight against the devil. They have prepared themselves in the fraternal line of battle for the single combat of the hermit. They have laid the foundation to fight, with the aid of God, against their own bodily and spiritual vices.

Third are the Sarabaites (the worst kind), unschooled by any rule, untested, as gold is by fire, but soft as lead, living in and of the world, openly lying to God through their tonsure (shaved heads). They live together in twos or threes, more often alone, without a shepherd in their own fold, not the Lord's. Their only law is the pleasure of their desires, and whatever they wish or choose they call holy. They consider whatever they dislike unlawful.

Fourth are the gyratory monks. All their lives they wander in different countries staying in various monasteries for three or four days at a time. They are restless, servants to the seduction of their own will and appetites, and are much worse in all things than the Sarabaites. It is better to be silent as to their wretched life style than to speak.

Casting these aside, let us with God's help establish a rule for Cenobites who are the best kind of monks.

CHAPTER 2:
The qualities of the abbot

To be qualified to govern a monastery an abbot should always remember what he is called (*Abba* = Father) and carry out his high calling in his everyday life. In a monastery he is Christ's representative, called by His name: "You have received the spirit of the adoption of sons, whereby we cry, Abba, Father" (Rom. 8:15). The abbot should not command, teach or demand anything contrary to the way of the Lord. But his orders and teaching ought to be tempered by Divine justice.

The abbot should always remember that he will be held accountable on Judgment Day for his teaching and the obedience of his charges. The abbot must be led to understand that any lack of good in his monks will be held as his fault.

However, he shall be held innocent in the Lord's judgment if he has done all within his power to overcome the corruptness and disobedience of his monks. Through his diligence and care he may say with the prophet: "I have not hidden Your righteousness in my heart; I have declared Your truth and Your salvation; but they have despised me and turned away" (Ps. 40:10). In the end death shall be given as a just punishment to those who have not responded to his care.

When a man is made abbot he should rule his monks by two principles: first, he should show them by deeds, more than by words, what is good and holy. To those who understand, he may expound verbally the Lord's directions: but to the stubborn and dull, he must exhibit the Divine commandments by his actions in his everyday life. If, by chance, he has taught his charges anything contrary to the law of God, he ought to clarify in his deeds that such things should not be done. For in his preaching he may be carried away and become a castaway, believing his own untrue words. If he has thus sinned, God shall not have to say to him: "Why do you declare my precepts and take my testament in your mouth? You have hated discipline and cast my speeches behind you" (Ps. 50:16–17). And "You who saw the splinter in your brother's eye, saw not the plank in your own" (Matt. 7:3).

The abbot shall not make distinctions among the people in the monastery. No one shall be loved more than others, except those who are found more obedient or observant in his faith. Unless there is good cause, the freeman should not be considered superior to the serf. If the abbot, after taking counsel with himself, finds such cause he may place the monk where he wishes in the order of precedence; otherwise let everyone stay in his own place for "whether bond or free we are all one in Christ" (Rom. 2:11) and are equal in the service of the Lord; with God there is no respecter of individuals. Only if we are found to excell in good works and humility are we preferred in the eyes of God as individuals. The abbot should love all equally, and let all be under the same standard of discipline according to that which each deserves.

In his instruction the abbot should always observe the apostolic rule: "Reprove, entreat, rebuke" (1 Tim. 4:2). As the occasion requires he should mix encouragement with reproof. He should show the sternness of a master and the love and affection of a father. He must reprove the unruly and undisciplined with severity, but he should exhort the obedient and patient for their own betterment. We warn him to reprove and punish the slothful and stubborn. He should not ignore the sins of offenders: but as soon as they appear and grow, he must root them out, remembering Heli, the priest of Silo.* He should verbally reprove the more virtuous and intelligent once or twice; but the stubborn, the proud, the disobedient and the hard-hearted should be punished with whips, even at the first signs of sin. For "The fool is not corrected by words" (Prov. 29:19). And "Strike your son with rod and you shall deliver his soul from death" (Prov. 23:14).

The abbot must always remember what he is and be mindful of his calling; he should know that the greater his trust, the greater the responsibility. He should recognize the difficulty of his position—to care for and guide the spiritual development of many different characters. One must be led by friendliness, another by sharp rebukes, another by persuasion. The abbot must adapt himself to cope with individuality so that no member of the community leaves and he may celebrate the monastery's growth.

Most important, the abbot must not undervalue or overlook the salvation of his charges. Thus he must always remember his task is the guidance of souls (for which he will be held accountable) and he must put aside the worldly, transitory and petty things. And if he complains of less abundant earthly goods, he ought to remember: "Seek first the kingdom of God, and His justice, and all things shall be given to you" (Matt. 6:33). And "Nothing is wanting to them who fear God" (Ps. 34:10).

He must prepare himself to account for the souls in his care; for on Judgment Day he will have to account for all his monks' souls, as well as his own, no matter how many. By fearing God's future questioning, he will be as concerned for his charges as he is for himself. He will

* 1 Kings 2, iv.

be cleansed of vice himself by helping others through admonition and correction.

CHAPTER 3:
The counsel of the brothers

Whenever an important matter is to be undertaken in the monastery the abbot should call the entire community together and should set forth the agenda. After hearing the various opinions of the brothers, he should consider all and then do what he thinks best. We feel that *all* should meet for the Lord often reveals the best course to a younger monk. The brothers should give advice with humility and not presume stubbornly to defend their views. They should leave the question to the abbot's resolution so that they may all obey that which he decides is best. But as disciples should obey a master, the master should arrange all matters with consideration and justice. Everyone shall follow the Rule as his master. No one should rashly deviate from it.

Individual desires have no place in the monastery and neither inside nor outside the walls should anyone presume to argue with the abbot. If he dares do so, he should be punished according to the Rule. The abbot himself must do everything according to the Rule and fearing God, knowing that he will be held accountable for his reign to the highest judge, God. The abbot should take counsel of the seniors alone in minor matters in the monastery for "Do all things with counsel, and you shall not regret it afterwards" (Eccles. 32:24).

CHAPTER 4:

The instruments of good works

1. To love the Lord God with all our heart, soul, and strength.

2. To love one's neighbor as oneself.

3. Not to kill.

4. Not to commit adultery.

5. Not to steal.

6. Not to covet.

7. Not to bear false witness.

8. To respect all men.

9. Not to do to another what one would not have done to oneself.

10. To deny oneself in order to follow Christ.

11. To chastise the body.

12. Not to love pleasure.

13. To love fasting.

14. To comfort the poor.

15. To clothe the naked.

16. To visit the sick.

17. To bury the dead.

18. To aid those in trouble.

19. To comfort the sad.

20. To reject worldliness.

21. To love Christ above all else.

22. Not to become angry.

23. Not to show temper.

24. Not to keep deceit in one's heart.

25. Not to make a false peace.

26. Not to forsake charity.

27. Not to swear, for fear of committing perjury.

28. To speak the truth with heart and lips.

9. Not to return an evil for an evil.
0. Not to injure anyone, but to accept patiently any injury oneself.
1. To love one's enemies.
2. Not to insult those who insult one, but to praise them.
3. To suffer persecution for the sake of justice.
4. Not to be proud.
5. Not to drink to excess.
6. Not to be a glutton.
7. Not to love sleep.
8. Not to be slothful.
9. Not to murmur.
0. Not to slander.
1. To put one's trust in God.
2. To attribute to God the good one sees in oneself.
3. To recognize that the evil in oneself is attributable only to oneself.
4. To fear Judgment Day.
5. To fear Hell.
6. To desire eternal life with all one's spirit.
7. To see death before one daily.
8. To monitor one's actions ceaselessly.
9. To know for certain that God sees all everywhere.
0. To dash one's evil thoughts against Christ immediately, and to reveal them to one's spiritual advisor.
1. Not to speak evil or wicked speech.
2. Not to speak much.
3. Not to speak idly nor so as to cause mirth.
4. Not to love boisterous laughter.
5. To enjoy holy reading.
6. To often partake of prayer.
7. To confess past sins to God daily in humble prayer and to avoid these sins in future.
8. Not to succumb to the desires of the flesh.

59. To despise one's own will.

60. To obey the abbot's commands in all things, even if he strays from his own path, mindful of the Lord's command: "What they say, do, but what they do, do not perform" (Matt. 23:3).

61. Not to desire to be called holy before the fact, but to be holy first, then called so with truth.

62. To fulfill God's commandments in one's activities.

63. To love chastity.

64. To hate no one.

65. Not to be jealous or envious.

66. To hate strife.

67. To evidence no arrogance.

68. To honor the elderly.

69. To love the young.

70. To pray for one's enemies for the love of Christ.

71. To make peace with an adversary before sundown.

72. Never to despair of God's mercy.

These are the tools of our spiritual craft. If we always remember and use them, and give them up only on Judgment Day, the Lord shall reward us as he promised, "Which eye has not seen, nor ear heard, nor has it entered into the heart of man to conceive what God has prepared for those who love Him" (1 Cor. 2:9). But the workshop in which we must diligently perform all these things is the seclusion of the monastery and our stability in the community.

CHAPTER 5:
Obedience

The first degree of humility is prompt obedience. This is necessary for all who think of Christ above all else. These souls, because of the holy servitude to which they

ave sworn themselves, whether through fear of Hell or
xpectation of eternity, hasten to obey any command of
superior as if it were a command of God. As the Lord
ays: "At the hearing of the ear he has obeyed me" (Ps.
7:44). And He says to the teacher: "He who hears you,
ears me" (Lk. 10:16).

These disciples must obediently step lively to the com-
anding voice—giving up their possessions, and their
wn will and even leaving their chores unfinished. Thus
he order of the master and the finished work of the dis-
iple are fused, with the swiftness of the fear of God—by
hose who deeply desire to walk in the path of the Lord.
hey walk the narrow path, as the Lord says: "Narrow is
he way which leads to life" (Matt. 7:14). They do not
ve as they please, nor as their desires and will dictate,
ut they rather live under the direction and judgment
f an abbot in a monastery. Undoubtedly, they find their
nspiration in the Lord's saying: "I come not to do my
wn will, but the will of Him Who sent me" (Jn. 6:38).

But this very obedience will be deemed acceptable to
God and pleasant to men only when the commands are
arried out without fear, laziness, hesitance or protest.
he obedience shown to superiors is, through them,
hown to God, who said: "He who hears you, hears Me"
Lk. 10:16). Orders should be carried out cheerfully,
or "God loves a cheerful giver" (2 Cor. 9:7). God will
ot be pleased by the monk who obeys grudgingly, not
nly murmuring in words but even in his heart. For even
f he should fulfill the command, his performance would
ot be pleasing to God who listens to his complainings.
Vork done in such a dispirited manner will go without
eward; in fact, unless he makes amends, he will suffer
he punishment meted out to gripers.

CHAPTER 6:
Silence

Let us do as the prophet says: "I have said: I will keep my ways so that I will not offend with my tongue. I have guarded my speech. I held my peace and humbled myself and was silent, even from speaking good things" (Ps. 39: 1–2). Here the prophet demonstrates that if we are not to speak of good things, for the sake of silence, it is even more vital that we not speak of evil lest we sin, for we shall be punished for that as a sin. No matter how perfect the disciple, nor how good and pious his speech he rarely should be given permission to speak for: "In much speaking, you shall not escape sin" (Prov. 10:19). The master should speak and teach, the disciple should quietly listen and learn. No matter what must be asked of a superior, it must be done with humility and reverent submission. We always condemn and ban all small talk and jokes; no disciple shall speak such things.

CHAPTER 7:
Humility

Holy Scripture proclaims to us brothers: "Everyone who exalts himself shall be humbled, and he who humbles himself shall be exalted" (Lk. 14:11). It tells us that all self-exaltation is a form of pride, against which, the prophet tells us, he guarded: "Lord, my heart is not exalted, nor are my eyes lifted up; neither have I walked in great things nor in wonders above myself. But to what purpose if I did not think humbly but exalted my soul? As a child weaned from his mother, so will you reward my soul" (Ps. 131:1-2).

Therefore, brothers, if we wish to reach the highest peak of humility and soon arrive at the heavenly heights, we must, by our good deeds, set up a ladder like Jacob's, upon which he saw angels climbing up and down. Without doubt, we should understand that climbing as showing us that we go up by humbling ourselves and down by praising ourselves. The ladder represents our life in the temporal world; the Lord has erected it for those of us possessing humility. We may think of the sides of the ladder as our body and soul, the rungs as the steps of humility and discipline we must climb in our religious vocation.

The first step of humility is taken when a man obeys all of God's commandments—never ignoring them, and fearing God in his heart. He must constantly remember that those who fear God will find eternal life while those who scorn Him will be cast into Hell. He must continually guard himself against all sins of body and spirit, and deny himself the fleshly lusts.

He should know that God sees him always. No matter where he is, everything he does is reported to God by the angels. The prophet proves this when he says that God is ever present in our thoughts: "God searches the hearts and mind" (Ps. 7:9). "The Lord knows the thoughts of men, that they are vain" (Ps. 94:11). Also, "You have understood my thoughts from afar" (Ps. 139:2), and "The thought of man shall confess to You" (Ps. 76:10). Let the prudent monk—so that he may avoid evil thoughts—always say in his heart: "Then I shall be spotless before Him, if I shall keep myself from my iniquity" (Ps. 18:23).

We are forbidden to do our own will for "Leave your own will and desires" (Eccles. 18:30), and "We beg the

Lord in prayer that His will may be done in us" (Matt. 6:10).

Thus we learn not to do our own will for Scripture warns us: "There are ways that seem right to men, but they lead, in the end, to the depths of hell" (Prov. 16: 25). We must fear what was said of the careless, "They have been corrupted and made abominable in their desires" (Ps. 14:1). And we must believe God is present even in our bodily desires, for, as the prophet says, "Lord all my desire is before you" (Ps. 38:9).

Thus we must guard against these evil desires, for death is near the doorway to pleasure. As Scripture commands us, "Chase not after your lusts" (Eccles. 18:30). Therefore, if "The Lord sees both good and evil" (Prov. 15:3), if He is always searching out the sons of men to find those who dwell on or seek God, and if our every move is made known to Him by the angels assigned to us—then, brothers, we must always be on the lookout, as the prophet warns us in the psalm. Let us fear that the Lord may say to us in the future, "Thus have you done, and I have been silent," if He should see us falling into evil ways and becoming useless—even though He may spare us for a while, because He is honorable and waits for us to reform.

The second step of humility is reached when a man, not loving his own will, does not bother to please himself, but follows the injunction of the Lord: "I came not to do my own will, but the will of Him who sent me" (Jn. 6:38). It is also said that "self-will has its punishment, necessity its crown" (*Acta Martyrum*).

The third step of humility is attained when a man, from love of God, obediently submits to a superior in imitation of the Lord. As the apostle says, "He was made obedient unto death" (Phil. 2:8).

The fourth step of humility is reached when a man, in obedience, patiently and quietly puts up with everything inflicted on him. Whether these are painful, unjust or even against his nature, he neither tires nor gives up, for the Scripture says, "Only he who perseveres to the end shall be saved" (Matt. 10:22) and "Let your heart be comforted, and expect the Lord" (Ps. 27:14). To show that the faithful must suffer all, no matter what, for the Lord's sake, the psalmist says, "For you we suffer death all day long; we are considered as sheep for the slaughter" (Ps. 44:22). Secure in the hope of Divine reward they rejoice, "But in all things we overcome by the help of Him Who has loved us" (Rom. 8:37).

Elsewhere the Scripture says, "You have tested us, Lord; You have tried us, as silver is tried, with fire. You have brought us into the snare; You have laid this tribulation upon our backs" (Ps. 66:10). And to show we ought to be subject to a superior, it adds immediately, "You have placed men over our heads" (Ps. 66:12). They fulfill the Lord's command in the midst of adversity and injustice—by the patience with which they obey: when struck on one cheek, they turn the other; when one takes away their coat, they let go their cloak also; when they are forced to carry a burden one mile, they go two; and with the apostle Paul, they suffer false brothers and endure persecution and bless those who curse them (Matt. 5: 39 ff.).

The fifth step of humility is achieved when a monk, by humble confession, discloses to his abbot all the evil thoughts in his heart and evil acts he has carried out. The Scripture tells us to do this: "Reveal your way to the Lord and hope in Him" (Ps. 37:5). Also, "Confess to the Lord because He is good, because His mercy endures forever" (Ps. 106:1). And the prophet says, "I have made known to You my offense, and I have not hidden my injustices. I have said, I will declare openly against myself, my injustices to the Lord; and You have pardoned the wickedness of my heart" (Ps. 32:5).

The sixth step of humility is reached when a monk contentedly accepts all that is crude and harsh and thinks himself a poor and worthless workman in his appointed tasks. He must say with the prophet, "I have been brought to nothing, and did not know it. I have become like a beast before You, and I am always with You" (Ps. 73:22-23).

The seventh step of humility is attained when a man not only confesses that he is an inferior and common wretch but believes it in the depths of his heart. He will humble himself and say, with the prophet, "I am a worm and no man, the reproach of men and the outcast of the people" (Ps. 22:6). "I have been exalted, and am humbled and confounded" (Ps. 88:15). And, "It is good for me that You have humbled me, so I may learn Your commandments" (Ps. 119:71).

The eighth step of humility is reached when a monk only does that which the common rule of the monastery or the example of his elders demands.

The ninth step of humility is achieved when a monk, practicing silence, only speaks when asked a question, for, "In many words you shall not avoid sin" (Prov. 10:19). And, "A talkative man shall not prosper upon the earth" (Ps. 140:11).

The tenth step of humility is reached when a man restrains himself from laughter and frivolity, for "The fool lifts his voice in laughter" (Eccles. 21:23).

The eleventh step of humility is arrived at when a monk speaks gently, without jests, simply, seriously, tersely, rationally and softly. "A wise man is known by few words" (Prov. 10:14).

The twelfth step of humility is reached when a monk shows humility in his heart *and* in his appearance and actions. Whether he is in the oratory, at the "work of God," in the monastery or garden, on a trip, in the fields; whether sitting, standing or walking—he must think of his sins, head down, eyes on the ground and imagine he is on trial before God. He must always repeat to himself, "Lord, I a sinner am not worthy to lift my eyes to heaven" (Lk. 18:13). And, "I am bowed down and totally humbled" (Ps. 38:8).

When a monk has climbed all twelve steps, he will find that perfect love of God which casts out fear, by means of which everything he had observed anxiously before will now appear simple and natural. He will no longer act out of the fear of Hell, but for the love of Christ, out of good habits and with a pleasure derived of virtue. The Lord, through the Holy Spirit, will show this to His servant, cleansed of sin and vice.

CHAPTER 8:
The Divine Office at night (Matins)[1]

During winter—from November first until Easter—the brothers shall rise at the eighth hour of the night as is reasonable; thus having rested a bit more than half the night, they will be refreshed. Any time left over ought to be used by the brothers to practice psalms or for reading.

From Easter until November first the hour for Matins should be arranged so that, after a very short break for going to the toilet, Lauds, which ought to be said at daybreak, may follow immediately.

CHAPTER 9:

How many psalms are to be said in the Night Office

In the winter, the Night Office should commence with the versicle "Lord, You shall open my lips and my mouth shall declare Your praise" (Ps. 51:15). This is chanted three times and is followed by psalms, said with a *Gloria*. Then Psalm 94 [95] with an antiphon is to be recited or sung, followed by a hymn, then by six psalms and their antiphons and a versicle.

After this the abbot should speak a blessing. All should then sit and three of the brothers should read, in turn, three lessons from the book on the lectern. After each lesson a responsory is to be sung, a *Gloria* following after only the last lesson. As the singer starts the *Gloria*, everyone will stand at once and all will bow their heads in honor of the Holy Trinity.

Both the Old and New Testaments are read at Matins along with commentaries by famous and orthodox Catholic Fathers.

After these three lessons and their responsories, six other psalms are to be sung with *Alleluias*. Then comes a lesson from the apostle, recited from memory, and finally a versicle and the prayer of the Litany—*Kyrie, eleison,* "Lord have mercy." Thus ends Matins.

CHAPTER 10:

How the Night Office is to be said in summer

From Easter to November first the same number of psalms laid down above is to be said. However, because of the short nights, no lessons are to be read from the book. In their place one lesson from the Old Testament will be recited from memory, followed by a short responsory. All else shall be as stated before. Make note that no fewer than twelve psalms, not counting Psalms 3 [3] and 94 [95], should be included in Matins.

CHAPTER 11:
How Matins is to be celebrated on Sundays

The brothers will arise earlier than usual on Sundays. Matins will be celebrated slightly differently. After the six psalms and the versicle have been sung, as prescribed above, the brothers will sit down by order of seniority. When this is done, one brother should read four lessons and responsories from the book. After the completion of the fourth responsory the cantor should sing the *Gloria* and all will rise in reverence.

After this, six psalms with antiphons and versicle will follow as before, and a further four lessons with responsories will be read. The abbot will choose three canticles from the prophets to be chanted with *Alleluias*. When the versicle has been sung, four lessons from the New Testament shall be read, according to the above order, the abbot's blessing coming before each.

After the fourth responsory, the abbot should begin the hymn *Te Deum laudamus*, and then he shall read with honor and respect a lesson from the Gospel while all stand. At the conclusion of the reading all will respond "Amen" and the abbot will chant the hymn *Te decet laus*. After the blessing, Lauds shall start.

This ordering of Matins on Sundays shall be followed in this way throughout the year. The only exception is if the monks—Heaven forbid—arise late; then the lessons or responsories may be shortened a bit. However, great care must be taken to see that this doesn't happen. If it does, the monk who was careless enough to permit it will make satisfaction to God in the oratory.

CHAPTER 12:
Lauds—celebration

At Sunday Lauds Psalm 66 should be said through without an antiphon. Then follows Psalm 50, with an *Alleluia*, Psalms 117 and 62, with *Alleluias*, the *Benedicite* (Dan. 3:52 ff.), the *Laudes* (Pss. 148 [148]–150 [150]), a memorized lesson from the Apocalypse, a responsory and hymn, a versicle, the canticle from the Gospel (*Benedictus*), the Litany (*Kyrie eleison*) and the conclusion.

CHAPTER 13:
Lauds—ordinary days

Lauds should be celebrated on ordinary days as follows: Psalm 66 [67] shall be chanted without an antiphon, as on Sunday, slowly though so that all may be in their places for Psalm 50 [51], to be chanted with antiphon. Then come two further psalms as follows: Monday, Psalms 5 [5] and 35 [36]; Tuesday, Psalms 42 [43] and 56 [57]; Wednesday, Psalms 63 [64] and 64 [65]; Thursday, Psalms 87 [88] and 89 [90]; Friday, Psalms 75 [76] and 91 [92]; Saturday, Psalm 142 [143] and the canticle from Deuteronomy, in two parts, each with a *Gloria*. Monday through Friday, the appointed canticles from the prophets will be chanted, as is the custom of the Roman

Church. After these, comes the *Laudes*, a lesson from the apostle (to be recited from memory), the responsory, hymn and versicle, the *Benedictus*, and the *Kyrie* and the conclusion.

Neither Lauds nor Vespers is to end without the Lord's Prayer, said aloud by the superior, in a voice all may hear because of the thorns of scandal always springing—so the brothers, remembering their pledge in the prayer: "Forgive us our trespasses, as we forgive those who trespass against us," may purge themselves. During the other offices, only the last part of the prayer is spoken, by the superior, so that all may respond, "But deliver us from evil."

CHAPTER 14:
Night Office on Saints' Days

On Saints' Days (feasts) and all Church festivals the Night Office should be carried out as on Sunday, the exceptions being that the psalms, antiphons and lessons are to be appropriate to these days. However, the order shall remain as before.

CHAPTER 15:
The seasons during which Alleluia is chanted

The *Alleluia* is to be sung with the psalms and responsories from Easter Sunday until Pentecost. From Pentecost until Lent commences, it will be chanted only with the last six psalms at Matins. However, on every Sunday (except during Lent) the Canticle, Lauds, Prime, Tierce, Sext and None will be chanted with an *Alleluia* only, and

Vespers with an antiphon. Responsories are only sung with an *Alleluia* from Easter to Pentecost.

CHAPTER 16:

The Day Office

The prophet says: "Seven times daily I have sung Your praises" (Ps. 119:164). We will cleave to this sacred number if we perform our monastic duties at Lauds, Prime, Tierce, Sext, None, Vespers and Compline. The same prophet says of the Night Office: "I arose at midnight to confess to You" (Ps. 119:62). In the Day Office, therefore, we ought praise our Creator for His just judgments, and at night we will rise to confess to Him.

CHAPTER 17:

The number of psalms said in the Day Office

We have decided the order of the psalmody for Matins and Lauds. Let us order the Hours which follow. Three psalms are to be chanted for Prime, each with a separate *Gloria.* An appropriate hymn is sung, before the psalms and after the versicle "O God, come to my assistance" (*Deus in adjutorium meum, etc.*). After the psalms a lesson from the apostle is recited, and the Hour is finished with the versicle, the *Kyrie* and dismissal. The Hours of Tierce, Sext and None are to be conducted in the same order as above.

If the monastic community is numerous, the Hours shall be sung with antiphons; if small, without. Vespers shall be chanted with an antiphon preceding and following each of four psalms. These shall be followed by a recited lesson, responsory, hymn, versicle, canticle from the Gospel, *Kyrie*, the Lord's Prayer and dismissal. Compline will be celebrated by the chanting of three psalms without antiphons, the proper hymn of the Hour, one lesson, a versicle, the *Kyrie*, the blessing and the dismissal.

CHAPTER 18:

Psalms—order to be chanted

In each Hour the versicle "O God come to my assistance; O Lord, make haste to help me" with a *Gloria* comes first, followed by the appropriate hymn. On Sunday four parts of Psalm 118 [119] are to be chanted at Prime. At Tierce, Sext and None three parts of Psalm 118 [119] shall be sung. On Monday, at Prime, only Psalms 1 [1], 2 [2] and 6 [6] are sung. Each day from Tuesday through Saturday, three further psalms are to be chanted through Psalm 19 [20]; so that Psalm 9 [9] and Psalm 17 [18] will each be divided and treated as two psalms. Thus, Sunday Matins will commence with Psalm 20 [21].

On Mondays at Tierce, Sext and None three parts of the remaining nine parts of Psalm 118 [119] shall be sung at each Hour. Thus Psalm 118 [119] will be completed on Sunday and Monday.

On Tuesday at Tierce, Sext and None the three psalms at each Hour will complete the nine psalms from Psalms 119 [120] to 127 [128]. These psalms are to be repeated at these Hours until the following Sunday. The order of hymns, lessons and versicles shall remain constant. Thus, on Sunday (at Prime) one will always start with Psalm 118 [119].

Four psalms are to be chanted every day at Vespers, starting with Psalm 109 [110] and ending with Psalm

147 [147], leaving out the psalms set aside for the other Hours (i.e., Pss. 117 [118] to 127 [128] and 133 [134] to 142 [143]). Since there will be three too few, Psalms 138 [139], 143 [144] and 144 [145] should be divided, while Psalm 116 [117], which is short, should be combined with Psalm 115 [116].

After the order of psalmody is arranged for Vespers, the lessons, responsories, hymns, versicles and canticles should be used as directed above. At Compline, Psalms 4 [4], 90 [91] and 133 [134] are to be repeated each day.

With the order arranged for the Day Office, the remaining psalms are to be divided among the seven Night Offices. The longer ones should be divided in half, and twelve should be permanently assigned to each Night Office.

If this arrangement is unsatisfactory to anyone, he may do otherwise if he has thought of a better one. No matter what, all 150 psalms must be chanted during the week so that on Sunday Matins the series may start afresh. Monks who chant less than the entire Psalter, with canticles, each week are slothful in their service to God. Our spiritual fathers performed with determination in one day what we now take a whole week to do.

CHAPTER 19:
How the Office should be performed

We believe that God is everywhere, and the Lord sees both good and evil in all places. Without doubt, we believe this is so especially when assisting in the Divine Office. Remember the prophet: "Serve the Lord in fear" (Ps. 2:10), and "Sing His praises with understanding" (Ps. 47:7) and also "In the sight of angels I will sing praise to

You" (Ps. 138:1). Let us consider our place in sight of God and of his angels. Let us rise in chanting that our hearts and voices harmonize.

CHAPTER 20:
Reverence at prayer

If we wish to ask a favor of those who hold temporal power, we dare not do so except with humility and respect. It is far more important that we present our pleas to God with the utmost humility and purity of devotion. We realize that we will be heard for our pure and sorrowful hearts, not for the numbers of our spoken words. Our prayer must be heartfelt and to the point. Only a divine inspiration should lengthen it. The prayer of the assembled community should be short. When the superior signals, all rise as one.

CHAPTER 21:
The deans of the monastery

In a large community respectable and devout brothers should be chosen and designated deans. They shall supervise their deaneries in everything according to God's commandments and the abbot's order. Deans should be capable of sharing the abbot's responsibilities. They should be chosen for their good character and their knowledge of men, not on seniority. If a dean becomes proud and vain on account of his office and is judged to blame, and if he is corrected for it three times and does not reform, then he should be removed from office and another brother put in his place. The same will hold true for the prior.

CHAPTER 22:

How the monks are to sleep

All the monks shall sleep in separate beds. All shall receive bedding, allotted by the abbot, appropriate to their environment. If possible they should all sleep in one room. However, if there are too many for this, they will be grouped in tens or twenties, a senior in charge of each group. Let a candle burn throughout the night. They will sleep in their robes, belted but with no knives, thus preventing injury in slumber. The monks then will always be prepared to rise at the signal and hurry to the Divine Office. But they must make haste with gravity and modesty.

The younger brothers should not be next to each other. Rather their beds should be interspersed with those of their elders. When they arise for the Divine Office, they ought encourage each other, for the sleepy make many excuses.

CHAPTER 23:

Excommunication for faults

If a brother is found to be stubborn, disobedient, proud or a murmurer, or at odds with the Holy Rule, or scornful of his elders' directions, he should be admonished by his superiors—in accordance with the Lord's injunction—twice in private. If even then he does not make amends, let him be reproved in public. However, if there is still no change, he shall be subject to excommunication, if he understands what kind of punishment this is. If he is obstinate he shall undergo corporal punishment.

CHAPTER 24:

The measure of excommunication

The severity of excommunication as a punishment depends upon the nature of the violation, which is to be judged by the abbot. For minor faults a brother should be kept from eating at the common table. This exclusion means that he shall not intone a psalm or antiphon or read a lesson in the oratory, until he makes his amends. His meals will be taken alone, after the others have finished. If the brothers eat at the sixth hour, he will do so at the ninth; if they eat at the ninth, he will eat in the evening. He will continue to behave like this until he has been granted pardon by means of some suitable act of atonement.

CHAPTER 25:

Grave faults

A brother guilty of a graver fault is to be excluded from the common table and the oratory. No one shall speak or meet with him. He shall work alone, remaining in penance and sorrow, and remembering the terrifying line of the apostle, "Such a one is delivered over to Satan for the destruction of the flesh, that his spirit may be saved in the day of the Lord" (1 Cor. 5:5). He shall eat alone, when and how much the abbot deems proper. He is not to be blessed as he passes nor is his food to be blessed.

CHAPTER 26:

Those who meet with the excommunicated without leave of the abbot

If a brother dares speak with or meet with the excommunicated brother, without the express permission of the abbot, he shall undergo the same penalty of excommunication.

CHAPTER 27:

The abbot's care of the excommunicated

The abbot must show great concern for the wayward brother for, "those who are well do not need the physician, but those who are sick" (Matt. 9:12). He must act as would a wise doctor and send a nurse to him—a wise elder brother who will console him as if by stealth and move him to humbly atone for his transgressions. This elder will comfort the transgressor to keep him from being overwhelmed by sorrow but, as the apostle says, "Let charity be confirmed in him and let all pray for him" (2 Cor. 2:8).

The abbot must take care, with diligence and cautious practical wisdom, not to lose any of his flock. He must remember that he has undertaken the care of sick souls, not the repression of healthy ones. Let him fear the Lord's words in the prophet: "What you saw to be fat you took to yourselves, and what was diseased you threw away" (Ezek. 34:3). He should follow the lead of the Good Shepherd who left ninety-nine sheep behind to search for the lost one. His compassion for weakness was such that

e stooped to place the sheep on his shoulders to carry it
back to the flock.

CHAPTER 28:
Those who do not change their ways despite much correction

If a brother does not change his evil ways, despite correction, even excommunication, then he must be punished
more severely—e.g., by whipping. If after this there is still
no change, or if in pride he defends his misconduct, the
abbot must behave like a wise physician. He applies the
salves and compresses of advisement, the medicine of the
Holy Scriptures and the hot iron of excommunication or
wounds of flogging. If even this has no effect, let him try
greater things—his prayers and those of the other brothers
—so that the Lord may cure the sick brother, for He can
do all things.

However, if all this is to no avail, the abbot must wield
the surgeon's knife. As the apostle says, "Put away the
evil one from among you" (1 Cor. 5:13), and "If the
faithless one depart, let him depart" (1 Cor. 7:15). Thus
the one sick sheep may not infect the flock.

CHAPTER 29:
Readmittance of departed brothers

A brother who has left the monastery, either through his
faults or by expulsion, and wishes to return must first
promise the complete amending of the fault. He may re-
enter but in the lowest rank so his humility may be put

to the test. If he leaves again, he may re-enter a third time.
After that he will be forever forbidden re-entry.

CHAPTER 30:
Correction of youths

Every age and intelligence should be treated in a suitable
manner. Youths who are at fault, or those who cannot
understand the gravity of excommunication, shall receive
just punishment (enforced fasting or flogging) so that
they may be healed.

CHAPTER 31:
The cellarer

One of the monks should be chosen cellarer—a man who
is wise, mature, sober, not gluttonous, not arrogant, not
argumentative, not disrespectful, not procrastinating and
not wasteful. He must fear God and be like a father to
the whole community.

He will take care of everything, but will do all under
the abbot's orders, making sure he does not offend any
of the brothers. If a brother makes an unreasonable request, he must not reject it out of hand but humbly and
reasonably turn it down.

He must look after his own soul, as the apostle says
"For he who discharges his service well shall win for himself a good place" (1 Tim. 3:13). He will care for the sick,
children, the poor and guests knowing for certain that he
will be held accountable on Judgment Day.

He will think of all the monastery's property as if they
were consecrated chalices. He must never neglect any o.

is charges, nor be greedy, nor lavishly wasteful of the
monastery's goods. He must do everything with restraint
and as the abbot directs.

Above all, he must have humility. If he has nothing to
give, his response (to the request) should be a good word
or, "A good word is better than the best gift" (Eccles.
18:17). Let him have under his care all that is delegated
to him by the abbot, but not what is another's province.
He will provide the brothers with their food allowance,
but without delay or arbitrariness, so they may not be
scandalized. He must remember what he might deserve:
"Who shall scandalize one of these little ones, it were better for him that a millstone be hanged about his neck,
and that he should be drowned in the depth of the sea"
(Matt. 18:6).

He should be given assistants if the monastery is large,
so he may perform his duties without worry. Things
should be both requested and distributed at convenient
times so no one will be bothered or upset in God's house.

CHAPTER 32:
Property and utensils

The abbot will choose brothers whose lives and virtue are
reliable to care for the clothes, tools and other monastic
property. He will give them charge of those things they
are to look after and collect when used, as he thinks best.
The abbot will keep an inventory, so that when other
brothers assume the task, the abbot may have an account-
ing. No one shall treat monastic property carelessly or in
a slipshod manner. If anyone does, he must be scolded,
and if no amends are made, he will be subject to the discipline of the Rule.

CHAPTER 33:
Private ownership by monks

The vice of private ownership must be uprooted from the monastery. No one, without the abbot's permission shall dare give, receive or keep *anything*—not book, table or pen—nothing at all. Monks have neither free will no free body, but must receive all they need from the abbot However, they may keep nothing unless permitted o given them by the abbot.

All things are to be common to everyone for, "Neither did any one say or think that anything whatever was hi own" (Acts 4:32). If any one is found with a predilection to this terrible vice, he is to be scolded twice. If he doe not reform, then he is to be punished.

CHAPTER 34:
The apportionment of necessities

"Distribution was made to everyone as was his need" (Acts 4:35). We do not mean by this that personal pref erence should play a part, but rather that individual weak nesses should be taken into account. He who has lesse need ought thank God and not lament. He who has grea need should show greater humility because of his weak ness and not gloat over the allowance made him. The everyone will be content. Under no circumstances shoul complaining be tolerated no matter what the reason. Any one found complaining should be subjected to most se vere punishment.

CHAPTER 35:
Weekly kitchen service

The brothers should wait on one another. No one is to be excused from kitchen duty unless he is ill or he is engaged in a task of greater import, for he can thus obtain greater charity and commendation. Depending on the size of the monastery and the convenient arrangement of the kitchens, let the weaker brothers have help to keep them from sorrow. The cellarer may be exempted from kitchen service in a large monastery, as may those engaged in more vital jobs as we have said. Let the remainder serve each other in charity.

After completing his weekly kitchen chores, the monk should clean on Saturday. He must wash the towels the brothers use for drying hands and feet. Everyone's feet are to be washed by the monk finishing his week's service and the one starting his. The monk ending service should return the utensils he has used clean and in good order, to the cellarer, who will then give them to the new kitchen staff. This is done so the cellarer may keep track of his inventory.

One hour before the meal each server may have a portion of drink and bread over his daily allowance, so he may serve his brothers without complaint or fatigue. The servers should wait until after Mass on feast days, however.

Right after Sunday Lauds both incoming and outgoing servers shall fall on their knees and ask for the prayers of all. When one finishes his week's service, he should say, "Blessed are You, O Lord God, who did help me and console me" (Ps. 86:17). When he has repeated this thrice, he shall receive a blessing. After this, let the one entering

his week of service say, "O God, come to my assistance
O Lord, make haste to help me" (Ps. 70:1). When this
has been repeated thrice by all, and the blessing received
these brothers may enter their week of service.

CHAPTER 36:
Sick brothers

Before others and above all, special care must be taken of
the ill so they may be looked after, as Christ, "I was sick
and you visited Me"; and "What you did for one of these
My least brothers, you did for Me" (Matt. 25:36, 40).

The sick must remember they are being taken care of
for the honor of God. They must not distress the brothers
who care for them with unreasonable demands. Nevertheless, these demands should be suffered patiently, since a
greater reward is obtained from them. The abbot must
ensure the sick are never neglected.

Let a separate cell be made available for the sick. The
infirmarian should be a God-fearing, compassionate and
attentive brother. The sick should be permitted baths as
often as necessary, but the healthy and especially all young
are to bathe rarely. The weak among the sick shall be permitted to eat meat to regain strength. When they are
cured, however, they must, by the Rule, abstain from
meat. The abbot will make sure the sick are not neglected
by the cellarer or the nurses for he is responsible for the
flaws in his disciples.

CHAPTER 37:
Old men and children

Human nature tends to show sympathy to the aged and to children. The Rule also should make provision for them. Their weakness will be considered and thus the Rule's directives on eating should be somewhat softened. They should be considered with kindness and be allowed to eat before commons.

CHAPTER 38:
The weekly reader

There should always be reading at the common meals. No one who picks up the book at random shall read. Rather, whoever starts reading on Sunday will continue for the entire week. After Mass and Communion, the reader will ask all to pray for him, that God may protect him from the sin of pride. In the oratory, he will chant, thrice, all repeating, "O Lord, You will open my lips, and my mouth shall declare Your praise" (Ps. 51:15). Then, he shall be blessed and start his weekly service. All will be silent at the table. No whispering or noise is to be heard, only the voice of the reader. The brothers should hand around food and drink so that no request is needed. If something is denied, then let it be asked for with a signal rather than verbally.

Also, no one is to ask questions about the reading or other things (for there would be occasions for idle chatter), unless the superior wishes to speak briefly for their moral improvement. The reader may have a draught of wine before commencing, on account of Holy Communion and because it might be too long for him to fast otherwise. He will eat later with the servers and kitchen staff.

The reading should not be done by all brothers in order, but only by those who may uplift the listeners.

CHAPTER 39:
Food apportionment

We believe that two cooked dishes will satisfy the daily needs at each meal—at the sixth and ninth hours. If some brothers cannot eat one, then they may eat the other. Two dishes must be enough for all. A third dish may appear if fresh fruit or vegetables are available. Whether it be eaten at one meal or two (dinner and supper), a pound of bread will be allotted to each monk daily. If supper is to be served, the cellarer will reserve a third of the ration for that meal.

If the monks have worked harder than usual, the abbot shall decree, if he thinks it wise, an increase in the ration. But care must be taken against excessive eating so that no one is laid low by gastric upset. Nothing is more contrary to being a Christian than gluttony. "Take heed to yourselves, lest your hearts be overcharged with surfeiting" (Lk. 21:34).

Young boys shall receive smaller portions than their elders—maintaining frugality in all. Except for the sick no one is to eat the flesh of quadrupeds.

CHAPTER 40:
Drink apportionment

"Everyone has his proper gift from God, one this, another thus" (1 Cor. 7:7). For this reason, we hesitate in apportioning others' food. If we are mindful of the sick, a *hemina* [¼ litre] of wine for each monk each day is adequate we believe. Those who have received the gift of abstinence will know they shall be especially rewarded by God.

Depending on local conditions, the strain of labor, or excessive heat more drink may be permitted at the will of the abbot. However, never let drunkenness and excess occur.

We read that wine is not for monks, but in our times they cannot accept this. Let us therefore agree on this limit at least, lest we satiate ourselves with drink. But, let us drink temperately: "For wine makes even the wise to fall away" (Eccles. 19:2).

If circumstances do not permit a full measure (or even any at all), the brothers shall bless God and refrain from complaining.

CHAPTER 41:
Dining hours

From Easter to Pentecost the brothers shall have dinner at the sixth hour and supper at night. From Pentecost through the summer the monks ought to fast until the ninth hour on Wednesdays and Fridays, provided that there is no field work and that the heat is not too great.

On other days they will dine at the sixth hour, or depending on conditions, at the discretion of the abbot.

Let the abbot temper and dispose all so that souls may be saved and the brothers' work may be performed without reason for complaining.

From September fourteenth until Lent dinner will be at the ninth hour. From Lent until Easter they shall dine in the evening.

Vespers should be timed so that the evening meal will be finished in daylight. No matter what (whether there be one meal or two), all meals should be finished in daylight.

CHAPTER 42:
No talk after Compline

Monks should try to speak as little as possible, but especially at night. This is true for all days—fast days or otherwise. If there are two meals, after supper they should sit together and one monk will read from the *Collations*, the *Lives of the Fathers* or something else uplifting. He will not read from the *Heptateuch* or the *Book of Kings*. It would not be good for weak souls to hear these readings at this time. They may be read at other hours.

If it is a fast day, after a short rest following Vespers, let them read from the *Collations*. Four or five pages shall be read, or as many as there is time for. During the reading all will gather, even those occupied with chores. Once they are all together they are to say Compline, after which no one is to speak.

If anyone speaks after Compline, punishment will follow. The only exceptions will be to accommodate the needs of a guest or if the abbot should give an order. This will be done with the greatest gravity and restraint.

CHAPTER 43:
Late-comers to the Divine Office and meals

Immediately upon hearing the signal for the Divine Office, all work must cease. Each monk will hurry to it, but with gravity. No frivolous behavior should ever occur. Nothing comes before the Divine Office.

If anyone arrives at Matins after the *Gloria* of Psalm 94 [95] (and on account of this the psalm should be chanted slowly), he is not to take his place in the choir. He shall go rather to the last place or someplace visible set aside by the abbot for dilatory monks so that all may see him. He will remain until after the Divine Office and make amends by public penance.

We have decided the above in order that the embarrassment will make them reform. If they remain outside the oratory they may fall asleep or indulge in idle chatter —thus giving the devil an opportunity. They must enter. Then they will not lose all, but will fare better in future.

At the daytime Hours he who dares not come to the oratory until after the versicle and *Gloria* of the first psalm will follow the rule above. He will not join the choir until he has made satisfaction. The only exception is when the abbot has given his permission, though under condition that he later make amends.

He who arrives late for meals (i.e., after the versicle) and thus neither prays nor sits down with his brothers, should be corrected twice. If he does not reform after this, he shall not be permitted at the communal meal but will eat separately and alone. He is to be deprived of his measure of wine also until he reforms and makes satisfaction. The same punishment applies to those who leave the meal before the closing versicle. No one is to eat or drink before or after the regular hours for meals. Should the superior offer something, let no one refuse. If he does refuse and then changes his mind (or wants something else), he shall receive nothing until he makes satisfaction.

CHAPTER 44:
How the excommunicated are to make satisfaction

He who has been excommunicated from oratory and the community table is to prostrate himself in front of the oratory door when the Divine Office is concluding. He shall lie there in silence, at the feet of the exiting brothers. He will continue this until the abbot has decided he has made satisfaction. When he enters the oratory at the abbot's bidding he will throw himself at the feet of the abbot and then the feet of the brothers, that they may pray for him.

He may then enter the choir and take his place, if and where the abbot directs. He must not take it upon himself to chant or read or do anything whatsoever in the oratory unless the abbot orders.

Also, after each hour of Divine Office, he is to prostrate himself where he stands. He will continue to do such until directed otherwise by the abbot.

Those excommunicated from the common table for a lesser transgression shall make satisfaction in the oratory as the abbot directs. They shall continue until he blesses them and declares the punishment ended.

CHAPTER 45:
Mistakes in the oratory

If one makes a mistake in chanting a psalm, responsory antiphon, or in reading a lesson, he must immediately humble himself publicly. If he does not, he will be more severely punished by his elders for he will not have corrected by humility what he did through negligence. Children should be whipped for these mistakes.

CHAPTER 46:
Offenses in other matters

If a monk while working does anything wrong, breaks or loses something or offends someone—in kitchen, cellar, garden, bakery, refectory, etc.—he shall go at once to the abbot and his brothers and confess, offering to make satisfaction. If he does not and it later becomes known, he shall be severely punished.

If the cause of the sin is secret (hidden in the soul), the monk should confess to the abbot or one of the spiritual fathers. They know how to heal their own and others' wounds in confidence.

CHAPTER 47:
Sounding the Hours of the Divine Office

The abbot shall have the responsibility, day and night, of calling the time for the Divine Office. He will give the signal himself or assign the task to a responsible brother. For all things ought be done at the designated hours.

After the abbot, the chanting of the psalms and antiphons is to be done in turn by those chosen. Only those
who can uplift the brothers shall sing or read. This will
be done with humility, gravity and reverence, and as the
abbot ordains.

CHAPTER 48:
Daily manual labor

Idleness is an enemy of the soul. Therefore, the brothers
should be occupied according to schedule in either manual labor or holy reading. These may be arranged as follows: from Easter to October, the brothers shall work at
manual labor from Prime until the fourth hour. From
then until the sixth hour they should read. After dinner
they should rest (in bed) in silence. However, should
anyone desire to read, he should do so without disturbing
his brothers.

None should be chanted at about the middle of the
eighth hour. Then everyone shall work as they must until
Vespers. If conditions dictate that they labor in the fields
(harvesting), they should not be grieved for they are truly
monks when they must live by manual labor, as did our
fathers and the apostles. Everything should be in moderation, though, for the sake of the timorous.

From October first until Lent, the brothers should
read until the end of the second hour. Tierce will then
be said, after which they will work at their appointed
tasks until None. At the first signal for None all work
shall come to an end. Thus all may be ready as the second
signal sounds. After eating they shall read or study the
psalms.

During Lent the brothers shall devote themselves to

reading until the end of the third hour. Then they will
work at their assigned tasks until the end of the tenth
hour. Also, during this time, each monk shall receive a
book from the library, which he should read carefully
cover to cover. These books should be handed out at the
beginning of Lent.

It is important that one or two seniors be chosen to
oversee the reading periods. They will check that no one
is slothful, lazy or gossiping, profiting little himself and
disturbing others. If such a brother is discovered, he is to
be corrected once or twice. If he does not change his ways,
he shall be punished by the Rule (to set an example for
others). Nor should brothers meet at odd and unsuitable
hours.

All shall read on Saturdays except those with specific
tasks. If anyone is so slothful that he will not or cannot
read or study, he will be assigned work so as not to be idle.

Sick and frail brothers should be given work that will
keep them from idleness but not so oppressive that they
will feel compelled to leave the monastery. Their frailty
is to be considered by the abbot.

CHAPTER 49:
Observance of Lent

A monk's life should always be like a Lenten observance.
Since few are capable of this, we urge that during Lent
we conduct our lives with the greatest possible purity.
Thus may we cleanse ourselves of all former negligences.
We shall do this worthily if we keep from all sin and devote ourselves to tearful prayer, reading, contrition and
abstinence.

During Lent we ought to add to our customary servitude: private prayer or abstinence from food and drink. Everyone, of his own will, should offer up to God, with joy of the Holy Spirit, more than is normal. He will deny his body in food, drink, sleep, talk and laughs. Thus he will look toward the holy feast of Easter with the joy of spiritual desire.

However, each monk must tell the abbot what he plans. It must be done with the abbot's blessing and consent, for if done without leave of the spiritual father it will be judged presumption and vainglory. It will thus be without worth. Everything must be done with the abbot's approval.

CHAPTER 50:
Brothers who work at a distance from the oratory or are traveling

Brothers who cannot come to the oratory at the appointed hours—because of their distant labor—should say the Divine Office where they are, kneeling in fear of God. The decision is to be made by the abbot.

Likewise, monks sent on a trip shall not neglect the Divine Office. They should say the Hours as best they can to fulfill their duty as servants of God.

CHAPTER 51:
Brothers who do not go far

A brother sent on an errand who expects to return to the monastery the same day is not to dine outside the mon-

astery. Even if asked by anyone, he will not, unless the
abbot has expressly ordered it. If he should do so, he will
be excommunicated.

CHAPTER 52:
The oratory of the monastery

The oratory is as its name signifies (a place for prayer).
Nothing else is to be done or discussed there. When the
Divine Office is finished all will leave in silence and with
reverence for God. Thus a brother who wishes to pray in
private will not be disturbed by anyone's misconduct.

If one wishes to pray alone at some other time, he will
simply go to the oratory and do so silently, with tears and
heartfelt fervor. Thus, as noted before, no one is to remain after the Divine Office, except for prayer, for those
who would remain and not pray are disturbing to their
brothers.

CHAPTER 53:
The reception of guests

All guests to the monastery should be welcomed as
Christ, because He will say, "I was a stranger, and you
took me in" (Matt. 25:35). Show them every courtesy,
especially servants of God and pilgrims. When a guest is
announced the superior or brothers should greet him with
charity; and they should pray together in order to be at
peace. The kiss of peace should not be given until after
prayer because of the deviousness of the devil. The greeting and farewell should be offered with great humility for

with bowed head and a prostrate body all shall honor in the guests the person of Christ. For it is Christ who is really being received.

Guests, after reception, are to be led to prayer. Then the superior or his delegate shall sit with them.

Let the Divine Law be read to the guest for his spiritual uplifting, and let every courtesy be shown him. Out of consideration for a guest a fast may be broken by a superior, except for inviolate days. Other brothers shall continue with their fast. The abbot will wash the guest's hands and, together with the brothers, his feet. Then they shall recite, "We have received Your mercy, O Lord, in the midst of Your temple" (Ps. 48:9). Special care should be taken of the poor and pilgrims for Christ is truly made welcome in them: wealth creates its own impression.

The kitchen of the abbot and guests should be separate from that of the community so as not to disturb the brothers, for the visitors, of whom there are always a number, come and go at irregular hours. Two competent and reliable brothers, appointed for a year, shall direct this kitchen. They will be given help when needed, to stem any complaints. Likewise, when they have free time, they are to work where directed. Indeed, this is true of all officers of the monastery: when they need help, they shall get it, but when they are free, they shall do as directed.

Let the guest room be cared for by a brother who fears the Lord. There should always be plenty of beds available. The House of God will be wisely governed by wise men.

No one may associate or converse with guests unless ordered. If one meets or sees a guest, he is to greet him with humility as we have said, and ask a blessing. If the guest speaks, the brother is to pass on, telling the guest that he is not permitted to speak.

CHAPTER 54:
The receipt of letters and presents

Without the abbot's permission a monk may not receive from or give to anyone, even his parents, letters or parcels. If his parents send him something he shall not dare receive it without first telling the abbot. But if the abbot has ordered it to be accepted, it lies in his power as abbot to give it to whomever he decides. The brother to whom it was sent should not be unhappy or hurt, giving the devil an opportunity. Anyone who would do differently shall be punished according to the Rule.

CHAPTER 55:
Clothing and shoes

Suitable clothing shall be given the monks, dependent on the climate. In cold regions more will be required than in warm. All this will be decided by the abbot. However, in temperate regions, we believe that each monk will make do with a cowl and tunic—heavy for winter, light (or worn) for summer. He should also have a shift for labor and shoes for the feet.

Monks should not complain of the color or texture of their clothing. It shall be whatever is available in the surrounding countryside or whatever is cheapest.

The abbot shall see to fit so that the clothes are not too short but properly sized to the wearer. When new clothes are handed out, the monks shall turn in their old ones. These will be stored in the wardrobe for the poor. Each monk needs only two each of tunics and cowls, so he will be prepared for night wear and washing. Anything else is superfluous and should be banished. Shoes and other garments will also be returned when replaced. Those who must travel are to be given leggings. Afterwards these are to be washed and returned. On these trips they should have better quality cowls and tunics than usual; these are to be returned after use.

Bedding shall consist of a mattress, coverlet, blanket and pillow. The abbot will make frequent inspections of the bedding to prevent hoarding. Any infractions are subject to the severest discipline and, so that this vice of private ownership may be cut away at the roots, the abbot is to furnish all necessities: cowl, tunic, shoes, stockings, belt, knife, pen, needle, towel and writing tablet. With these, any excuse for need will be vanquished.

The abbot must always remember, "And distribution was made to everyone according to his need" (Acts 4:35). He should take into account the frailties of those in need and not the hostility of the envious. In everything he should think of the retribution of God.

CHAPTER 56:
The abbot's table

The abbot will eat with guests and travelers. When there are few guests he may invite any of the brothers to dine with him. However, a couple of the seniors should always be with the brothers for the maintenance of discipline.

CHAPTER 57:
Artisans and craftsmen

Craftsmen present in the monastery should practice their crafts with humility, as permitted by the abbot. But if anyone becomes proud of his skill and the profit he brings the community, he should be taken from his craft and work at ordinary labor. This will continue until he humbles himself and the abbot is satisfied. If any of the works of these craftsmen are sold, the salesman shall take care to practice no fraud.

The salesman must remember Ananias and Sapphira unless they—or others who dispose of monastic property dishonestly—wish to suffer the death of their souls as well as their bodies. In pricing, they should never show greed, but should sell things below the going secular rate. Thus God will be glorified in all things.

CHAPTER 58:
The admission of new brothers

Admission to the religious life should not be made easy for newcomers. As the apostle says, "Try the spirits if they be of God" (1 John 4:6). Should the petitioner continue knocking [on the gate], and if he shows patience and persists in his petition for several days despite harsh treatment and reluctance to admit him, he shall be permitted lodging in a guest room. After a few days he shall move into the novitiate. He shall meditate, eat and sleep there.

A senior, skilled in conversion, should supervise him to

see if he truly seeks God and eagerly hopes for the Divine Office, obedience and humiliations. He must be told of the difficulties and austerities ahead of him on the pathway to God.

If he promises to continue and persevere, the Rule shall be read to him at the end of two months. He will be told: "Behold the law under which you wish to fight. If you can observe it, enter upon the life; if not, you are free to leave."

If he remains firm in his conviction, he will return to the novitiate and be tested again with patience.

After six months more the Rule should be read to him again so he may know what he's getting into. If he continues, the Rule shall be repeated to him after four months more. If after much thought he promises to follow the Rule and obey his superiors, he will be received into the community. He must know that he is now under the law of the Rule, that he cannot leave the monastery nor live without the Rule, for he has had time to decide one way or the other.

Upon admission, in the oratory, before all, he is to promise before God and His Saints to be stable, obedient and to live as a monk. Should he act otherwise, let him know that he will be condemned by God whom he mocks. He shall make his promise in the name of the saints whose relics lie there and to the abbot. He is to write this out with his own hand. If he is unlettered, another shall do this for him, and he shall make his mark upon it and place it on the altar with his own hands.

After this, he shall begin the versicle "Accept me, O Lord, according to Your promise, and I shall live, and let me not be confounded in my expectation" (Ps. 119:116). Everyone shall repeat this (after him) three times, at the end adding, "Glory be to the Father, etc." The novice will prostrate himself before each monk, asking for his prayers.

From this day on he will be considered a member of the monastery.

If he owns anything, he must either give it to the poor beforehand, or deed it to the monastery, keeping nothing for himself, for he now owns nothing, not even his own body.

When this is done he is to change his clothes for those of the community. His old clothes are to be kept in the wardrobe for if he should be persuaded by the devil to leave the monastery, he will be stripped of his habit and expelled. His written profession will not be returned, but rather kept by the abbot in the monastic records.

CHAPTER 59:
Sons of noblemen or of poor men offered to God's service

When a nobleman offers his son to God's service in the monastery, if the child is under age, the parents should write out a petition as above. They should wrap this, along with their offering, and the boy's hands in the altar cloth, dedicating him to God.

As concerns property, the parents must give their oath in the document that they will give him nothing nor allow him the chance to receive something from them or anyone else. If they prefer, they may give what they wish as a free gift to the monastery, reserving the income if they wish. All this shall be managed so the child has no expectations, from which, experience has shown, he may be misled and perish in the eyes of God.

Those who are poor are to act in the same manner. And those with nothing shall simply make the deed and offer their son before witnesses.

CHAPTER 60:
Priests who would live in the monastery

Should a member of the priesthood wish to enter the monastery, permission is not to be immediately granted. If he persists in his desire, he must know that he shall have to obey the Rule strictly. No exceptions are to be made, for, as Scripture says, "Friend, for what are you come?" (Matt. 26:50). However, he shall be allowed to rank after the abbot, to give the blessing or say Mass if ordered by the abbot. He shall not presume to do so otherwise since he is subject to the discipline of the Rule. He must give to all examples of greater humility.

If there arises a possible appointment to an office, or to other monastic work, let him take the rank at which he entered the community, not that which is conceded to him from the reverence for the priesthood. Lesser members of the clergy desiring entry into the monastic life will be placed into a middle rank, providing they promise adherence to and stability in the Rule.

CHAPTER 61:
Reception of pilgrim monks

A stranger (monk) from a distant locale may be received as a guest for as long as he desires providing he does not make unreasonable demands but accepts the ways of the brothers and is satisfied. If he thinks something wrong and points it out humbly, charitably and judiciously, the abbot should circumspectly meditate upon it, for the Lord may have sent the stranger for that purpose. If he desires to remain permanently, he should not be refused for during his stay as a guest his behavior and devotion will have been judged.

If he has been mean and disruptive, he should not be permitted to become a member of the community, but rather openly be asked to leave so as not to be a bad influence. However, if he is not deserving of expulsion, he shall be admitted to the community as a full member upon request. In fact, he should be persuaded to stay so others may be taught by his good example. For in every place we serve the same Lord and we fight under the same King.

If such a monk is found deserving by the abbot, he may be given a higher rank. The abbot may also promote those clerics and priests deserving of it. However, the abbot must never receive permanently a monk of another monastery without consent of that monk's own abbot or letters of reference. It is written, "What you will not have done to yourself, do not to another" (Matt. 7:12).

CHAPTER 62:

Priests of the monastery

Should the abbot wish to have a priest or a deacon ordained, he should choose from among his own monks. Those chosen must be worthy of the priesthood. The ordained monk must be neither arrogant nor proud. He must not do anything other than what the abbot orders, for he is even more subject to the Rule's discipline. He should never use his office as an excuse to stray from the Rule's obedience and discipline, but must forever strive to reach God.

He will keep his entrance rank except in service at the

altar, or if the worthiness of his life prompts the community to recommend and the abbot to direct his promotion. Despite this he must follow the rules laid down by the deans and provosts. If he does not he will be judged a rebel, not a priest. If he does not reform though admonished, the bishop should be called as a witness. If even then he does not change his ways, and his bad conduct is known by all, he shall be expelled from the monastery. But this should only happen if his inflexibility is such that he will not submit to the Rule.

CHAPTER 63:
Rank in the monastery

The brothers will rank in order, depending upon the date of their entrance, the merit of their lives or the order of the abbot. The abbot must not disrupt his charges or arbitrarily shift their ranks by the misuse of power. He must remember that he is accountable to God for all his decisions and deeds.

In whatever order the abbot directs or which is theirs by seniority the brothers shall receive the kiss of peace, approach Communion, intone the psalm and take their places in the oratory. In all cases order shall not be prejudiced by age, for Samuel and Daniel, but youths, sat in judgment of the priests.

With the exception of those promoted or demoted by the abbot, everyone shall take his place by the date of his entrance to the monastery. For example, one who entered the community in the second hour shall be junior to one who entered in the first hour, no matter his age or former position. Children should be kept under strict discipline by all.

Thus the juniors will honor their seniors, and the seniors, love the juniors. In speaking, one shall not merely use the other's given name. The senior shall call the junior *Brother*, the junior shall call the senior *Father*. The abbot, however, since he takes the place of Christ, shall be called *Abbot* or *My Lord*. This is done out of honor and love of Christ, not because of his assumption of dignity. The abbot must remember this and act so as to be worthy of such honor.

When brothers meet, the junior shall ask a blessing from the senior. When a senior passes, the junior will get up and offer his seat. The junior will not sit until asked to by the senior, for it is written, "In honor they prevent one another" (Rom. 12:10).

Youths should always stay in place at the communal table and in the oratory. Outside, no matter where, they should be kept under strict supervision until they come of age.

CHAPTER 64:
Election of the abbot

Always remember, concerning the election of an abbot, that he should be chosen by the entire community, in fear of God, or, if that proves unsatisfactory, by part of the community, however small, who would choose more rationally. The abbot should be chosen for his virtue and wisdom, even if he ranks lowest in the community.

If the community elects someone who encourages their wickedness, and this is made known to the bishop of the diocese or other abbots and good Christians in the locale, these in turn should annul the choice. And they should choose a worthy overseer of God's House. They shall be rewarded for this if it is done through love of God and with pure heart. If they neglect their duty they will be punishable for sinning.

The newly elected abbot must ponder his great responsibilities and remember to Whom he must render account. He is to know it is better to profit others than to rule over them. He must be knowledgeable in Divine Law so as to know when to "bring forth new things and old" (Matt. 13:52). He must be virtuous, sober and merciful, and always hold mercy before justice; thus he may obtain mercy. He shall hate vice and love the brothers.

He shall act with prudence and moderation as concerns punishment, for if a pot is scoured too vigorously to remove rust, it may break. Let him remember his own frailty, for "the bruised reed must not be broken" (Is. 42:3).

We do not intend that he allow vices to grow. He must weed them out with prudence and charity, as each case demands. He should try to be loved, more than feared. Neither must he be worried or anxious, nor too demanding, obstinate, jealous or oversuspicious; for he will never have peace.

When he gives an order, spiritual or temporal, let it be done prudently and considerately. In all he orders he should show discretion and moderation, thinking of Jacob, "If I shall cause my flocks to be driven too hard, they will all die in one day" (Gen. 33:13). Taking up the mother of virtues, discretion, he should temper all things so that what the strong may wish and the weak not flee may be the state of affairs.

He will follow the present Rule in all matters. Thus, administering it wisely, he may hear from the Lord what the good servant who gave grain to his peers in due season heard: "Amen, I say to you, over all his goods will he place him" (Matt. 24:47).

CHAPTER 65:
Provost of the monastery

Often the appointment of a provost gives rise to grave scandals in the monastery. There are some who, at times —bloated with arrogance and playing abbot—act like tyrants and bring about scandal and dissension in their community. This often happens in places where the provost is appointed by those who choose the abbot. Such a one may easily be turned to anything absurd because from the very beginning he is given matter for pride, while his imagination lets him think he is not under the power of the abbot, because the same men have chosen both of them.

From this arise envy, quarrels, slanders, jealousies, rivalries and mayhem. And while the abbot and provost are at odds it follows that their souls are in jeopardy from their quarrels. Likewise, those under their direction, by siding with one or the other, are paving the way to their own destruction. The fault for this condition must lie with those responsible for the appointments in the first place.

Thus, for the preservation of peace and charity all offices in the monastery, we feel, should be in the disposition of the abbot. As we have said previously, all monastic concerns should be managed by the deans as the abbot has decided. With several in charge, no one will have the opportunity to become proud.

However, if the community humbly requests or the place requires a provost, the abbot, with the counsel of God-fearing brothers, shall appoint one if he thinks such appropriate. The provost will take care to faithfully carry out his appointed tasks, never contradicting the directions or will of the abbot. The higher a monk is raised above his brothers, the more careful he must be to follow the Rule.

If the provost shows himself to be a man of fault, or proud, turns against the Holy Rule, he shall be verbally admonished four times. If he does not make amends he shall be subject to regular discipline. If he still refuses to reform, let him be removed from office and another, worthier, be put in his place.

After all this, if he refuses to be quiet and obedient, he shall be expelled from the monastery. Nevertheless, the abbot must remember that he will have to account to God for all his decisions, and he should thus guard his own soul against envy and jealousy.

CHAPTER 66:

The porter of the monastery

A wise old monk should guard the gates of the monastery. He shall know how to receive and answer a question, and be old enough so he will not be able to wander far. His cell should be nearby; thus, all who arrive will find someone to give information.

When someone knocks, or a poor man calls, the porter shall answer, "Thanks be to God," or ask for a blessing. With all the courtesy of the fear of God, he should reply to a question humbly and with charity. If he needs help (in his duties) he should be given a younger assistant.

The monastery should be planned, if possible, with all the necessities—water, mill, garden, shops—within the walls. Thus the monks will not need to wander about outside, for this is not good for their souls. We wish this Rule to be read frequently to the community so none may plead ignorance and make excuses.

CHAPTER 67:
Brothers sent on a journey

When brothers are about to undertake a journey, they should ask the prayers of the community and the abbot. All brothers who are away from the monastery should be remembered in the closing prayers of the Divine Office.

On the day of their return, they should prostrate themselves at the completion of each Hour of the Divine Office and ask the prayers of the entire community for any sins they may have committed by seeing or hearing evil, or by idle chatter.

No one shall recount his adventures outside the monastery because this is most harmful. Violators will be subject to regular punishment. Anyone who leaves the monastery, goes anywhere, or does anything, however small, without the abbot's permission will be similarly punished.

CHAPTER 68:
When a brother is asked to do the impossible

If a brother is requested to do something difficult or impossible he should, at first, accept the command meekly and obediently. If he sees that the task is beyond his means, respectfully, calmly and humbly, he will tell his superior the reason for it. He will not be proud, resistant or contradictory.

If the superior keeps to his decision despite the brother's reasons, the brother in charity will do as told, trusting in God's help.

CHAPTER 69:
No one shall presume to defend another in the monastery

Take care that, no matter what, no monk presumes to defend or protect another, not even if they share a familial relationship. No monks shall be permitted to do this in any manner, for it can lead to scandal. Anyone who does shall be severely punished.

CHAPTER 70:
No one is to presume to strike another

No occasion for presumption shall be allowed in the monastery. We insist that no one is to strike or excommunicate a brother unless ordered by the abbot. Anyone who breaks this rule shall be publicly reprimanded, so all may be in fear.

Children under fifteen shall be under strict discipline and constant care by all, but moderately and with discretion. Anyone who dares do this to older monks, or is hard on children beyond all good sense (without the abbot's order) shall be subject to the discipline of the Rule, for it is written, "What you will not have done to yourself, do not to another" (Matt. 7:12).

CHAPTER 71:
The brothers ought to obey one another

The service of obedience is to be shown to all, not just the abbot, for by this road of obedience they shall travel to find God. The orders of the abbot and of his superiors come first; no others are to be preferred. Juniors shall obey seniors in charity and with care. Anyone who disputes orders ought to be punished.

If a brother is corrected by the abbot or his superiors, no matter for what, he shall prostrate himself and offer satisfaction until he receives a blessing; likewise if he realizes he has angered or disturbed a superior in any way, he should do the same. Anyone who refuses to do this shall be whipped, and if he remains unreformed, let him be expelled from the monastery.

CHAPTER 72:
The good zeal monks should possess

There is evil and bitter rivalry which keeps one from God and leads to Hell. Likewise there is a good spirit of zealousness which keeps one from vice and leads to God and eternal life.

Monks should practice this zeal with ardent love. Let them, "in honor prevent one another" (Rom. 12:10). Let them accept each other's frailties (of body or soul). Let them try to outdo each other in obedience. Let no one do what is best for himself, but rather what is best for another. Let them expend the charity of brotherhood in chaste love. Let them love their abbot with sincerity and humility. Let them fear God and think of nothing before Christ, Who can lead us into eternal life.

CHAPTER 73:
All perfection is not herein attained

We have composed this Rule so that, through its observance in monasteries, we may know we have made some progress in pursuit of virtue and the commencement of a monastic life. For those who are hurrying to attain a truly holy life, there are the works of the Holy Fathers. The following of these will lead a man to heights of perfection. For what page or word of the Bible is not a perfect rule for temporal life? What book of the Fathers does not proclaim that by a straight path we shall find God? What else but examples of the virtue of good living, obedient monks are the *Collations, Institutes, Lives* of the Saints, of the Holy Fathers, and the Rule of St. Basil? We who are slothful, bad living and careless should be ashamed. Whoever you are, if you wish to follow the path to God, make use of this little Rule for beginners. Thus at length you will come to the heights of doctrine and virtue under God's guidance. Amen!

Notes

CONFERENCES and INSTITUTES   John Cassian, who had developed his ideas of monastic living in the communities of Bethlehem and the Egyptian desert, brought these ideas to Marseilles when he founded his Monastery of St. Victor there. His near neighbor, Bishop Castor (in Apt, forty miles north of Marseilles), had asked Cassian for advice and assistance in translating Egyptian monastic ideals for would-be monks in the harsher climate of Gaul. Between A.D. 419 and 426 Cassian wrote for Castor (and for his own monks at St. Victor) the twelve-book *Institutes for Monasteries and the Eight Remedies Against the Eight Capital Vices* and the twenty-four *Conferences of the Fathers*.

The *Institutes* dealt with the rules and customs of the Egyptian monastic practice and suggested means for combatting the eight vices Cassian saw as most destructive of the monastic ideal. The *Conferences* were interviews (probably composite, fictionalized accounts) with the most well known of the hermits living in the Egyptian deserts. These contained sound spiritual advice on various general and particular questions.

EUCHARISTIC FAST   The person who wished to receive the sacrament of the Eucharist, the body and blood of Christ under the appearances of bread and wine (consecrated at the celebration of the Mass), was expected to observe a complete fast from food and drink before doing so. Since the reader began his duties immediately after the conclusion of the Mass with no time to eat before doing so (Chapter 38), he was allowed the mixture of water and wine as a means of sustaining his strength. In addition, his drinking of the draught would complete his consumption of the sacrament and prevent any of its particles from being profaned.

EXCOMMUNICATION The excommunication prescribed by the *Regula* as punishment and penance for faults against the Rule and violations of monastic discipline was patterned after, but not identical with, the exclusion from the sacramental life imposed by the Church upon flagrant violators of Divine or Church law. Benedict's excommunication was of two kinds. The severity of the fault and the dispositions of the transgressor, as judged by the abbot, determined whether the less or the more severe punishment was imposed.

The lesser form of excommunication (Chapters 24 and 44), separated the monk from the activities of the community by placing between him and his brethren spatial and temporal distances. The delinquent took his meals alone and three hours later than the rest of the community. During the chanting of the Divine Office, he was not allowed to stand in his regular place in the choir, but had to stand apart in an area designated by the abbot for such penitents—a kind of "penalty box." Further, he was forbidden to take a public role in the chanting, e.g., intoning a psalm, reading a lesson.

The more severe form of excommunication (Chapters 25–28, 44), completely isolated the delinquent monk from the life of the community. He performed his assigned tasks alone, was served unblessed food and ate it alone, was not allowed inside the oratory for the Divine Office but had to stand silent outside the door, and, still silent, had to prostrate himself as the community left, to beg their prayers and blessing. Further, no one in the community, except the abbot, was allowed to speak to him, even to give him a greeting or a blessing. Anyone who made any move to contact him was liable to the same punishment.

The duration of either form of excommunication was at the discretion of the abbot who had the additional option of keeping the information to himself, thus adding uncertainty to the transgressor's other pains. Before the transgressor was restored to his place in the community, and to full participation in its activities, he had to prostrate himself at the feet of the abbot and his brethren to beg forgiveness and the abbot's blessing. He also had to demonstrate over the period of his punishment penitence for his faults, a change in the dispositions which had caused them and a firm resolve to amend. Here, as in the imposition of the punishment, the abbot was the judge.

LITURGICAL SEASONS Life in the cloister was shaped both by the seasons of the year and by the Church's liturgical seasons of penance and joy. There were two basic patterns, the Winter Order and the Summer Order, according to which the work and prayer of the Benedictine life were arranged.

The Winter Order included the Church's chief penitential season, the forty-day fast of Lent, which served as preparation for the spring feast of the Resurrection, Easter. In the Winter Order manual labor was performed during the morning hours with spiritual reading, study of the psalms and similar activity split in two periods, one just before the day's work began, and one between the conclusion of the main meal (served at the ninth hour) and Vespers. (See *opus Dei* for an explanation of the arrangement of the Divine Office.) Lent pushed the hour of the one meal of the day to after Vespers, with a lengthened period of spiritual reading before the work of the day was begun.

The Summer Order began with the feast of Easter.

From Easter to Pentecost, a period of fifty days, no fast was allowed, and the monks had a midday and an evening meal. From Pentecost to the start of the Winter Order (September 14), fasting was resumed with the main meal eaten at the ninth hour on Wednesdays and Fridays (traditional fast days in the early Church), and at the sixth hour on other days. Manual labor in summer was performed in the cool of the morning and late afternoon, with reading and rest in the midday heat.

OPUS DEI—THE "WORK OF GOD" The "work of God" (*opus Dei*), later known as the "Divine Office," was a duty each monk took upon himself as he officially entered the life of the monastery. As Benedict prescribed it, the *opus Dei* consisted of eight periods of formal, oral, communal prayer spaced throughout the day and night. Psalms, hymns, and readings made up the bulk of each period of prayer or Hour (*hora*).

The day began with "vigils," or the Night Office (now called Matins), which was prayed at roughly 2 A.M. The Day Office began with the second period of prayer, held at daybreak. This hour was at first called Matins (*Matutini*) from the time of its performance—in the early morning. It soon came to be called Lauds from its usual recitation of the "praise" psalms (*Laudes*), Psalms 148–50.

The hours of Prime, Tierce, Sext, and None were recited during the first, third, sixth, and ninth hours of the day respectively, according to the ancient methods of reckoning time. That is, these hours were prayed at approximately 6 A.M., 9 A.M., 12 noon and 3 P.M., depending upon the season.

The seventh period of prayer, Vespers, was timed to end at sundown and the rising of the evening star. Compline ended the Day Office and the day, as darkness fell.

STABILITY   Stability is one of the conditions Benedict saw as essential to the proper regulation of the Christian monastic life. By a vow or promise of stability, a monk too'. upon himself the obligation of remaining within ʲue physical boundaries of the monastery which had accepted, by the hands of its abbot, his profession of religious commitment.

Stability benefited the individual by giving him spiritual "roots" and a family of brothers to replace those he had renounced in leaving the world. It benefited the community by ensuring a relatively fixed population, living under a single rule interpreted by a single authority, and pledging themselves to persevere in that state until death. If members of one monastery were commanded by their abbot to found a new house in another place, their vows of stability were transferred to the new foundation.

TONSURE   Tonsure is a ceremonial shaving of the head, sometimes in the form of a cross, by which a person signifies his renunciation of the world and its vanities for a life of penitential asceticism.

MONASTIC BUILDING The plan and construction of the monastery is a historically complicated problem, varying enormously as to location, size, requirements and philosophy. Virtually nothing remains from Benedict's own period in the West, but we can say with some conviction that a cenobitic monastery would be built as a compound containing the monks' cells, refectory, kitchen, guest house and oratory or church. Such so-called "typical" plans as St. Gallen were neither typical nor widespread. They were ideals and pretty much remained that way. By the Carolingian period (c. 800–900), monasteries had enlarged their domains and their functions. Thus there might be cloisters for contemplation, libraries for study, *scriptoria* for the manufacture of books, shops for carving and casting, a smithy, storerooms, mill, granary, barns, animal pens, cellars, wine presses—the implements and division of labor that would characterize a small, self-sufficient town or manor. The important thing to remember is that, except for the foundation houses, most of the monasteries were small. Cluny at its peak housed four hundred; the average was probably fewer than fifty. Numbers in the Middle Ages are always smaller than we would wish. Even including the lay brothers, who eventually become a factor in planning, there were as many people as in a summer resort in winter.

LIVING CONDITIONS To the modern reader, the conditions under which a monk was to live seem harsh and severe. However, if we consider the social and economic situation at the time the *Rule* was composed—the very end of Roman administration of the greater part of Europe—the life of a monk takes on more pleasant and wholesome connotations. True, he was placed under strict limitations, but it must be remembered that the limitations on the outside were, due to circumstances and whim, usually far more severe. At least a monk was fed regularly, clothed in sturdy garments and treated with some degree of fairness and respect. The peasant in the field was lucky to get one meal a day, was subject to the ravages of battle and the hostility of his neighbor. And the monk was, in his own mind, much further along the path to Salvation.

Composite Plan of a Medieval Benedictine Monastery

A. Oratory (church)
B. Dormitories (cells)
C. Abbot's house/library
D. Lavabo (wash house)
E. Refectory (dining hall)
F. Stores/brewery
G. Kitchens
H. Animal pens
I. Well
J. Guest-house/stables
K. Gatehouse

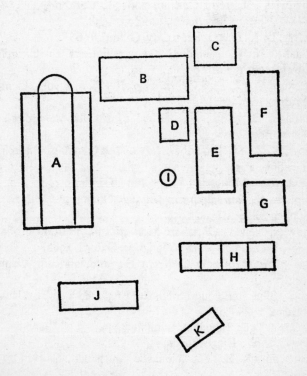

Further Reading

The literature on monasticism is enormous. We have listed below a few books, accessible in most libraries, we feel will be useful for gaining more detailed knowledge. They are all in English.

Brooke, Christopher, *The Monastic World*, New York, 1974.

Butler, Cuthbert, *Benedictine Monachism*, London, 1919.

Chadwick, O., *John Cassian*, 2nd ed., Cambridge, 1968.

——, *Western Asceticism*, London, 1958.

Chitty, D. J., *The Desert a City*, Oxford, 1966.

Conant, K. J., *Benedictine Contributions to Church Architecture*, Latrobe, Pa., 1949.

Coulton, C. C., *Five Centuries of Religion*, 4 vols., Cambridge, 1923–50.

Cranage, D. H. S., *The Home of the Monk*, 3rd ed., Cambridge, 1934.

Cross, F. L., ed., *Oxford History of the Christian Church*, London, 1957.

Evans, Joan, *Monastic Life at Cluny*, London, 1931.

Hilpisch, S., *Benedictinism through Changing Centuries*, Collegeville, Minn., 1958.

Knowles, David, *Christian Monasticism*, London, 1969.

——, *From Pachomius to Ignatius*, Oxford, 1966.

——, *The Monastic Order in England*, 2nd ed., Cambridge, 1963.

——, *The Religious Orders in England*, 3 vols., Cambridge, 1948–59.

McCann, J., *St. Benedict*, London, 1939.

New Catholic Encyclopedia

Swartwout, R. E., *The Monastic Craftsman*, Cambridge, 1932.

Wormald, F., *The Monastic Library*, London, 1958.

Zarnecki, George, *The Monastic Achievement*, New York, 1972.

A more detailed critical bibliography can be found in Christopher Brooke, *The Monastic World* mentioned above.

OTHER IMAGE BOOKS

OTHER IMAGE BOOKS

A 88-2

OTHER IMAGE BOOKS

OTHER IMAGE BOOKS

A 88-4

OTHER IMAGE BOOKS

A 88-5

OTHER IMAGE BOOKS

YOUR CATHOLIC WEDDING: A Complete Plan Book – Rev. Chris Aridas

A 88-6